Father and Sons

Melina Balistreri

Copyright ©2024
All rights reserved. Written permission must be secured from the author to reproduce any part of the book.

Printed in the United States of America

ISBN: 979-8-3304-3366-7

10 9 8 7 6 5 4 3 2 1

EMPIRE PUBLISHING
www.empirebookpublishing.com

Dedication

In memory of my mother, my father, my grandparents,
and with the rest of the family.

ACKNOWLEDGEMENTS

I want to thank my grandchildren Kelsey, Sabrina and Adriana, and my daughters Mary Lou and Margaret for helping me translate my book from Italian to English.

Prologue

Don Nino is a very elegant, intelligent, and courageous man. He is very well respected by everyone. He is a man of business; he knows what he is doing and what he wants. He loves his family immensely. The last word is supposed to be his, and everyone must obey him. He works very hard and honestly and makes a lot of money. He is married, and he loves his wife, Concetta. Sometimes, he believes that he is the happiest man in the world. He has everything: love, money, good health, and success in his work. The destiny of each of us, nobody knows how, where, or when it comes, and it gives us a surprise especially when we least expect it.

Don Nino, in a short time, would lose his wife and the baby they were expecting. For him, everything would come crashing down. With the passing of time, he would marry a second time, to lose his second wife, leaving behind five kids. When he thought he would not get married again, he instead married for a third time. Together with his third wife, they had one son, and they were together for a long time. Don Nino has always been a very strong man, and while he already has enough problems, he was not expecting what would happen with his sons Salvatore and Bastiano.

This storm with his sons is long, interesting, dramatic, sad, and pensive. As you read this book, you will find out what's going to happen. In this life, there is joy and pain, and we must face it. Don Nino has been having a lot of adventures of joy and suffering. He has a gift from God to have good health and live a long life.

Father and Sons

Chapter 1

Conca D'Oro is a beautiful island in Sicily. The island is known for its balmy Mediterranean weather, the fecundity of its rich earth, the clarity of its sunlight, and the pungent odors of its native lemon and orange blossoms.

There, you will find a small town near Palermo called San Nicola L'Arena, located near the ocean and the mountains.

This community had roughly seven hundred citizens in the early 1900s. It is filled with close, mostly related families.

Everywhere you look, you will see stone houses whose red-tiled roofs are bathed daily by the sun's liquid gold. Each balcony is redolent with the perfume of assembled flowers, with jasmine being the most prominent.

This community did not live peacefully among each other and would fight to survive.

Sicily was a land where men killed each other with the same ferocious enthusiasm felt by a torero when killing a bull.

This murderous madness between families would often commence over something as trivial as the ownership of an olive tree.

Neighbors might even kill each other over the amount of water one would take from the communal stream.

A man could even be murdered due to perceived disrespectful behavior or comments made regarding someone's wife or daughters.

Not everyone believed in this culture of violence, but even the cool-headed head of the Mafia succumbed to the general madness, which resulted in many wars to the death.

Many town residents were concerned for their family's safety because of the endless violent quarrels that harmed everybody.

This changed suddenly when Don Nino LoBuono brought the warring factions to peace.

After his parents' death, Don Nino decided to sell their Villa in Bagheria. He then built a house between his brother, Salvatore, and his sister, Anna Maria, in San Nicola. He chose to keep the great land of olive trees and vineyards.

Don Nino purchased more land near the mountain to help make wheat. On one part, he would rent to a farmer who raised cows and sheep. This farmer also produced butter, milk, sieno cheese, ricotta, parmesan, and other products daily.

Instead of collecting rent, Don Nino amassed a large quantity of homemade products.

Getting the Sicilian people to vote was challenging, even if they were offered compensation.

They believed in self-help and revenge, not in an elected government. Even Mussolini admired and applauded his proceedings against the Mafia.

The New York Times wrote an article titled "THE MAFIA DEAD, A NEW SICILY IS BORN." But they were wrong. The Mafia in Sicily never died, and it certainly hadn't ended.

The great Italian hero of the Risorgimento, Giuseppe Garibaldi, briefly served as dictator of the island. In Sicily, the Mafia helped run the community. The Mafia was more powerful than anything else.

The American government decided to use the Mafia organization in Sicily, which Mussolini and Mori had forced into inactivity. But it was still very much in existence.

The ruler of the Mafia in the Allied invasion of Sicily was not yet chosen. The Mafia helped to hamper the resistance of the Italian Army.

When WWII started, Mussolini could no longer give Sicily his attention.

The Mafia took this opportunity to quietly open a line of communication with other divisions of their business, sending messages of hope to the Mafia.

During this time, the US Army arrived in Italy. Don Nino extended his helpful hand to the American soldiers, allowing them to find refuge in his land.

Don Nino sent wine, bread, fruit, cheeses, and many other offerings to help feed the soldiers. In return, the American soldiers would help him to protect his family.

The American Army accomplished its mission ahead of schedule with minimal loss of life.

CHAPTER 2

During the fall months, Don Nino would make olive oil from the olive trees and sell it to the community's people.

On the vineyard property, he produced wine from the grapes and sold it to the community during the winter months.

Don Nino was a great farmer who knew how to run a business like his grandfather. He also farmed every fruit and vegetable that was sold at the local markets in the local communities.

Don Nino went on a trip to New York to visit his godfather, Mancini. While he was there, he met a beautiful woman named Concetta.

His godfather gave him his blessing and indicated that Concetta had a wonderful family. They happened to also be from Sicily.

Concetta and her family were from Cerda, two hours from San Nicola, where Don Nino lived.

Concetta kept in close contact with her sister Maria and her brother Calogero, as well as with her parents.

After Concetta and Don Nino had been married for two years, they found that Concetta was expecting.

They were excited and content with their upcoming blessing as they awaited the arrival of their first child.

The expectant mother could not contain her desire to inform her family in New York about the wonderful news.

Don Nino & Concetta

Concetta's family wrote to her and, in their eagerness, convinced Concetta that she and Don Nino should sail to New York.

For Concetta, they claimed the trip would be like a vacation. Don Nino was working hard and was preoccupied with his affairs.

Concetta tried to convince her husband to make this cruise seem like the reality of a beautiful dream.

"Sarebbe un sogno diventare realtà. Come godersi un'alba o un tramonto e vivere l'emozione di una tempesta. Partecipare all'idea di vivere un'esperienza nuova senza preoccupazioni e immergersi completamente nella natura," she said to her husband.

For her, it would be like living a beautiful dream life, a break from the pressures and cares of daily life. It would be a dream fulfilled at last.

It took quite some time of Concetta requesting to take this trip, but Don Nino was finally convinced by his wife.

He said to her, "Yes, I want to please you. I will do my best, but it will be difficult for me because I must leave some of my men in charge of the businesses during my absence."

Don Nino went and spoke with several of his henchmen. He said, "You will need to do my work for a month because my wife wants us to visit her family in New York. If any of you have problems, you must inform me of them."

The next day, Don Nino and his wife began preparing for the trip. In April, the happy couple parted from Palermo on the liner Saturnia, with the destination of New York.

The first several days of the voyage brought temperate weather.

Don Nino and Concetta were content to be together, relaxing on the luxurious ship and looking forward to arriving to visit the family.

But after three days had gone by, the weather started to change.

The sea became very agitated, and the ship rocked back and forth, upsetting the balance of the passengers.

Finally, the captain and the commander ordered all passengers to remain in their cabins to avoid people being knocked down on the unstable deck and possibly injured.

Already pregnant for three and a half months, Concetta had begun to feel sick.

Don Nino was very concerned about Concetta's condition and attempted to help his wife as best he could.

But Concetta was very ill. She was unable to keep any food or drink in her stomach and was vomiting continuously.

The weather stayed ugly, and the ship remained unsteady. Concetta felt worse each day that passed.

There were two doctors on board the ship who tried to do everything they could to save Concetta and her unborn child.

Upon seeing the grave condition of his wife's health, Don Nino realized it was a bad idea to have followed her wishes regarding a transatlantic cruise.

Don Nino and Concetta were so happy and content with their beautiful marriage and the upcoming arrival of their first child. But the cruel hand of fate had decreed that Concetta would not arrive in New York alive.

Don Nino was exhausted by the loss of his wife and unborn child. He felt sad and guilty about accepting the idea of making this trip.

He was both upset and displeased. He could not help but think that they should have just waited for Concetta to give birth before making the long trip.

He thought, "What will I say to my wife's family now that she is dead? The loss of both my wife and my baby has shaken my life."

However, he could not avoid the need to explain what had happened to Concetta's family.

When he finally arrived in New York, Concetta's family was already at the port, anxiously awaiting their arrival.

One can only imagine the feelings of Concetta's mother, as well as the rest of her family, upon learning about the sudden death of their daughter and the baby she was expecting.

They were all incredibly sad and wept that their beloved daughter had arrived in New York dead. They wanted to know what the circumstances of her death were.

Don Nino explained the difficult weather conditions that disrupted the previously smooth course of the voyage and how Concetta had been taken sick because of this.

He asked his in-laws for forgiveness, stating that he did not want her to make the trip to America due to her pregnancy condition.

"Concetta was so excited to come see her family here in New York that she did everything possible to convince me to say yes, and she finally succeeded," explained the bereaved husband.

"Now, I am full of regret for allowing myself to be convinced by her to make this long journey, and now it is too late. There is nothing that I can do."

Don Nino further elaborated, "My life, which was previously so happy and full of love with my wife at my side and expecting a child, has now become a tragedy in only one week."

"I will remain here in New York until after the funeral. I cannot stay here after that because my heart grieves for my loving wife who is no longer with me and for the child that I will never meet," cried Don Nino from the depths of his broken heart.

However, Concetta's father, Luigi Chiappone, tried to convince his former son-in-law to stay a while longer.

"Nino, there is no need for you to go just yet. Please stay with us for at least a few more days. We can reminisce about Concetta and how happy she made you. Talking about her would be good emotionally for both you and us."

Thus, Don Nino was convinced to remain in New York with his in-laws for one month.

One day, while they were eating dinner, Concetta's mother, Lucia, asked Nino if he would chaperone her other daughter, Maria.

"While you are still here with us, you could accompany Maria when she leaves the house. Who knows, you might enjoy it."

Nino replied that although he would be glad to fulfill this request, he would only do so to please Lucia.

"At the moment, I do not feel the need to be out in the world. Rather, I wish to remember my dead wife and recall all our happy times together."

He continued, "However, Donna Lucia, you are like a second mother to me. So, to please you, I shall go and accompany Maria when she must go out of the house."

After having accompanied Maria on her excursions over several days, Nino's feelings of sadness began to deepen due to the intense physical resemblance between the living girl and her dead sister.

For days, this feeling of sadness developed into a soft melancholy.

Upon seeing the melancholy state into which her brother-in-law had declined, Maria, a sensitive soul, asked him one day, "Nino, what can I do to lighten the burden you carry with you? I do not like to see you in such a melancholy frame of mind."

Nino replied, "The only way to please me would be if you could give me back my beloved wife. Since I know that this is impossible, there is nothing that anybody can do to help me."

Maria kissed him gently on the cheek and said, "Yes, there is something that I can do for you. You are a very handsome man and so noble, sincere, honest, and courageous."

She continued, "Anyone who would have the pleasure of knowing you would certainly fall in love with you, and your life will change for the better."

Don Nino replied, "What are you saying, Maria? I do not want to marry again because I am in too much pain due to the loss of my beloved wife."

Maria responded, "You are wrong, Nino; you must make a new life and be happy again. Concetta would have wanted this for you, and I will help you. In these few days that you have taken me out, I have fallen in love with you."

She continued, "I know it will be difficult for you, but in time, I believe you may develop feelings for me, too."

Don Nino was speechless at Maria's words. When they returned to Maria's home, she spoke with her family and announced that she would be going with Nino to Sicily.

Maria's mother enthusiastically responded, "We are happy to hear this!"

As she turned to Nino, she said, "Marry Maria before you return to Sicily; that way, you will be part of our family."

She continued, "We all love you. I believe that Maria will make you very happy, and she will give you many children!"

She continued, "But remember, never allow her to travel when she is pregnant."

Because Maria so deeply resembled Concetta, Nino decided to marry Maria before returning to Sicily.

Once Nino and Maria were married, they made the journey back to Sicily.

Nino arrived home and went back to his work in his various businesses. After three months, Maria found that she was pregnant. She could not wait to tell her husband the good news that she was expecting his child.

When Maria told Nino the news, he was so happy and excited. However, he was very worried about what happened to Concetta and their baby.

He promised Maria that he would do everything in his power to assure her and their baby's health.

During her pregnancy, Maria took very good care of herself and finally gave birth to a healthy baby girl. They named her Marietta.

Don Nino was happy that things went well and he finally had a family. Two years later, Maria gave birth to their first boy. They named him Salvatore.

Don Nino was ecstatic to have a son who would grow to learn every aspect of the business. Finally, he would have someone he could trust.

Don Nino and Maria had three more children. Sebastiano, Salvatrice, and Francesca.

Don Nino was proud and content. He had the family he always wanted.

Maria was terribly busy raising five children, but she never complained because she loved them and loved having her big family.

Even though Maria never complained, Don Nino surprised her one day by hiring a nanny to help her.

Maria Chiappone (Second Wife) with her five children.

Chapter 3

In the middle of the small town of San Nicola, there was a large piazza.

Once a year, Don Nino would use the piazza for his wheat. He would place large tents on the stony ground, and they would fill one tent with the harvested wheat.

Because of the extreme heat, Don Nino would put dark glasses and hats on the horses and mules to try and keep them cool.

Don Nino installed a pole in the middle of the tent, and he would tie the horses and mules to this pole. As the animals walked around the pole, their hooves stomped on the wheat to separate the kernels from the sheaf.

In the second tent, ten women were employed to sift the wheat. The sifted wheat would be sent to the mill where it was made into flour.

That year, Nino's wife was expecting another child. However, this time, the pregnancy was perilous, and the doctor indicated that Maria should remain in bed, stay calm, and rest. But once again, cruel destiny took a hand.

There was an extremely sweltering day, and while the animals were stomping the wheat on this very hot day, they began slowing down. They were tired.

Don Nino's son Bastiano was six years old. He was at the piazza and wanted to help his father with the animals.

Bastiano was close to one horse, and with a stick in his hand, he waved it around, trying to make the horse go faster.

Instead of the horse going faster, the horse panicked and went into a wild gallop, which caused a big commotion.

Bastiano then tried to calm the horse down, but this angered the horse. The horse reared, stomping on Bastiano, who fell to the ground.

Because he was so frightened, Bastiano did not move. He was so still that everyone assumed the worst, that he was severely injured or even dead.

From a short distance, where all the houses were located, Marietta's godmother saw what the horse did to Bastiano, who was no longer moving. She thought he was dead.

She stupidly ran to Don Nino and Maria's house and called out, "Commare! Commare! The horse has killed Bastiano."

Her reaction caused Maria to jump out of bed as Maria cried, "Oh no! It cannot be true! Oh, God, please help!" But before Maria could even see what happened, she collapsed to the floor.

Marietta, the eldest daughter, ran to Don Nino and said to him, "Papa, please come home quickly. Mamma has fallen, and she is not well."

Marietta continued, "My godmother told mamma that the horse killed Bastiano. Mamma got very upset and jumped out of bed because she wanted to see what was happening. But she fell on the ground before she could do so. Papa, we need you."

"Where is Bastiano? Is it true what my godmother said?" Marietta asked.

Don Nino replied, "No, my child, Bastiano is fine. Do not worry."

He then told her, "When he fell, he was fortunately not injured. But because of what happened, he was too frightened to move and laid still on the ground."

Don Nino continued and told his daughter, "Commare Giovanna should not have done this because she frightened your mother."

Don Nino quickly calmed down the horse, left some of his men in charge of continuing the work, and ran towards home, which was fortunately near the piazza.

After arriving home, Don Nino lifted his wife off the floor and gently placed her back onto the bed.

Don Nino said to his wife, "Tesoro, what Commare Giovanna told you is not true at all. Bastiano fell to the ground, but he was not injured. He is perfectly fine."

He continued, "Now, you need to rest. I am going to call the doctor, and you will see that everything will be okay."

"Thank you," replied his wife.

The doctor arrived one hour later. After examining Maria, he told Don Nino, "Maria is very weak. She lacks the strength to even get up or to try to walk."

"Make sure that she has plenty of rest, and we will see how she feels tomorrow. The child is fine, " the doctor said.

When the doctor returned the following day, he found that Maria was weaker than the previous visit. She was so lethargic that she lacked the strength even to speak now.

The doctor turned towards Don Nino and said, "Be strong! Only a miracle can save your wife now. I am sorry to give you such unwelcome and unfortunate news."

"The frightening news which the Commare gave to your wife caused Maria to go into a shock. The shock she received caused a disturbance to her blood system," the doctor continued.

"Stay close to her and give her courage. If you need me, call me any time."

Don Nino never left his wife's side by day or by night. He did not even think about his work.

He prayed that Jesus would perform a miracle so that he would not lose his second wife.

But after two more days, Don Nino saw that Maria was extremely pale; her eyes were always closed, and she stopped eating.

Cruel destiny had, for the second time, taken a wife away from Don Nino. Maria died the following day, leaving behind her five children and leaving her husband without a wife.

Marietta was the eldest child, being nine years old at the time of her mother's death. The youngest child, Francesca, was only two years of age.

After the funeral, Don Nino continued to work and contracted a woman to help him care for the children so that he could continue working.

While working, he could not help but think that destiny had taken away from him two wives. Not just two wives but two wives who had been sisters.

He felt sad that he had lost the mother of his children and that his children no longer had a mother. He dedicated all his time to his children and his work. Such is life. We cannot prepare for what destiny may bring us.

Regardless, we must keep going forward even if we are sad. Sometimes, we must think about those loved ones no longer with us. It is important to recall the happy days we spent with them.

CHAPTER 4

A year later, in the small town of Porticello, near San Nicola, lived a family well known to the Commare Giovanna Dugo. Giovanna knew that the husband of this family, 42-year-old Carmelo Rizzo, was dead.

There was a widow, Maria D'Aquisto, who had one six-year-old child. Maria had a sister named Lucrezia, who lived in Brooklyn, New York.

When Lucrezia discovered that her sister was now a widow, she began arranging the paperwork for Maria to come live with her in America.

In the meantime, Giovanna, who felt terrible guilt because of her actions that caused the shock to Maria, wanted to remedy what she had done by helping her Compare Nino.

Therefore, she decided to visit her Compare, Nino.

The first thing she said to him was, "Forgive me, Compare, for what I did. I was stupid, ignorant, and impulsive without thinking about the possible consequences of my actions. I am sorry for what happened, and if you forgive me, I have some news to give you."

Don Nino responded, "I have despised you since the day Maria died. Because of you, I lost my wife, and my children lost their mother."

He continued, "A year has passed, and I have never stopped thinking about my wife. Even with a caretaker for my five children, it is not the same. She is not their mother, and she is not my wife. Unfortunately, life keeps going. And I have been thinking about forgiving you. So, what is this news you have for me?"

Giovanna responded, "I know a widow in Porticello. Her husband died six months ago, and she has a six-year-old girl named Fortunata. Her name is Maria D'Aquisto."

"She has a sister in America who has prepared paperwork for her to immigrate to America," Giovanna continued.

"When she told me what was going on, I thought of you. With your permission, I want you to meet her. If you would like, you could marry her, and she can help you with all the children."

Don Nino responded, "It would be a pleasant occasion if she would also like to meet me."

He continued, "Let me know when you can arrange for us to meet so I can get to know her. We will see from there."

Giovanna made the trip to Porticello to visit Maria a few days later.

They exchanged greetings, and Maria told Giovanna, "My sister has almost everything prepared so that I can go to America with Fortunata in about a month. We have been friends for a long time, and I am very sad to have to leave you."

Giovanna responded, "I also have some good news for you. I do not think you need to go to America; you can stay here in Sicily."

"I know a good-looking and wealthy man who lost his wife a year ago," Giovanna continued.

"He has five children and is looking for a wife and second mother to help raise them. He is terribly busy with his work, and he told me that if he gets married to a proper wife, he will give her the power to manage his money. So, what do you think, Maria?

Would you like to meet him? If yes, we will go to visit him together, and you can tell me what you think of him."

Maria spent a few minutes thinking about her daughter's future. "Okay, Giovanna," she responded, "I would like to meet him, and then I will give you my answer."

Giovanna returned to San Nicola to see Don Nino. "Maria agrees to meet you," she says to him.

After one week, with Giovanna's help, Don Nino prepares a beautiful dinner for Maria and her daughter. They could spend the occasion getting to know each other.

That Sunday, Maria and Fortunata arrived in San Nicola. Don Nino, his children, and Commare Giovanna welcomed them with warm greetings. When it was time to eat, they all sat down.

As the first to speak, Don Nino looks at Maria and says, "First, I want to thank you for coming and meeting me. I find you incredibly attractive and intelligent."

"You are a good woman with a good daughter who will be wonderfully comfortable with my children," he continued.

"We will all respect the two of you if you choose to stay with us. So, whenever you are ready, I would like to know how you feel about this."

"Even though you have five children, you are a very good-looking man," responds Maria.

"Please allow me two weeks to write to my sister in America and discuss this with her before I give you an answer. I would also like to talk with my daughter about how she feels as well."

Don Nino agrees, "Ok, I understand. We will see you in two weeks."

Maria and her daughter returned to Porticello.

Maria begins thinking, "I will speak to my sister, but I will be the one who makes this decision."

She speaks to Fortunata, but she does not understand its significance because she is only six years old.

All she could think about was playing with Don Nino's children.

Fortunata says to her mother, "Yes, mamma, I want to go back to that man's house!"

As Maria listens, she begins writing a letter to her sister in America:

Dear Sister,

I am writing to tell you the news since we last spoke.

My daughter and I are okay, and I hope the same for you and everyone else there. I thank you for everything you have done for Fortunata and I.

Until a few days ago, I was excited to come to America, though everything has changed.

A friend introduced me to a good-looking and wealthy man. He invited my daughter and I to his house and introduced us to his children.

His name is Lo Buono Antonino. He has five children, and his wife died a year ago. He was very impressed with me and I him. I am sorry to tell you, but I have decided not to come to America. I hope you understand and agree with me.

I send hugs and kisses, as well as from my daughter, to you and your family.

Please write back as soon as possible so I know how you feel about this.

Your Sister,
Maria

Lucrezia & Husband

After ten days, Maria received a letter from her sister, which she read expectantly:

Dear Maria,

Everyone here is anxiously awaiting the arrival of you and your young daughter. I read your letter and understand everything you wrote to me. We are disappointed with your decision.

I was informed about Antonio L.B. You are correct: He is handsome and wealthy.

However, you need to realize that he has five children, and if you marry him, you will have many worries about raising his five children in addition to your own daughter.

Maria, I think it will be hard and extremely difficult for you. You are not their mother, and you do not know how they will treat you.

Right now, they are young, but when they are older, you cannot predict what will happen in the future. I suggest that you think about this carefully.

I want to help you, but you are the one who decides. I hope that you make the right choice. I love you very much and wish only the best for you and your daughter.

Write to me as soon as you have decided.

Ciao for now,
Your Sister Lucrezia.

Maria decided to respond to her sister with a letter.

Dear Lucrezia,

I got your letter. Thank you for what you wrote me. I love you, too. I have decided to marry Don Nino. I believe that my daughter and I will have a good future. Thank you for all you have done for us and for understanding me. I hope you forgive me for deciding not to come to you to America. We will stay in touch, and I will tell you about everything that is going on. I will end this letter by sending you many kisses from me and my daughter to you and your family. I will write to you soon,

Your Sister, Maria

After two weeks, Maria returned to San Nicola to inform Don Nino about her decision to marry him.

Don Nino was happy to learn the news and, hugging her, said enthusiastically, "Grazie, Maria! You will not regret this."

Maria said to Don Nino, "While the children are growing, I will teach them to be close to the family, to be both honest and sincere, to love each other, and to help each other when necessary."

She continued, "They must also learn to treat my daughter Fortunata as if she were another sister and to respect me."

"I know that I cannot take the place of the mother your children have lost, but I promise you and them that I will do the best I can. I am sure you will be happy with me."

Don Nino and his children were all satisfied with what Maria had said.

After being acquainted with each other for two months, Don Nino L.B. and Maria D'Aquisto married.

They had a wonderful wedding party. Everything went very smoothly. The children had a lot of fun. They got along well with each other and played very happily together.

After the marriage, Don Nino honored his promise to Maria that she would be allowed to manage all the money earned through his various businesses.

3rd Wife – Maria D'aquisto

CHAPTER 5

After two years of marriage, Don Nino and Maria were blessed with a baby boy. The children were happy because now they had another companion to play with.

For Fortunata, the birth of a baby brother was an especially joyous occasion because she now had a sibling who was related to her by blood rather than merely by the ties of marriage.

For the first four years, the marriage was a happy one. Everything went well, and everyone was happy and content.

Suddenly, one day, everything changed. Don Nino, speaking with his wife, said to her, "Maria, I have decided that in the future I want my son Salvatore to marry your daughter Fortunata so that the property will remain in the family. What do you think about this?"

Maria, stunned, replied "That is not possible. They grew up together, and they love each other as siblings. I do not know what my daughter will think when she is older since they have been siblings for four years."

She continued, "They love each other, but it is not the type of love that leads to marriage."

Arrogantly, Don Nino replied, "Then, the two children must be raised in different households and no longer be near one another. This will help us reach our plan for them to get married eventually."

Maria was very unhappy with this revelation of her husband's plans for her daughter's future, but she understood that what her husband wanted could not be resisted.

Therefore, she said that she would speak with her daughter about Don Nino's intentions. She spoke with her daughter but mentioned nothing about what Don Nino had said about the marriage to Salvatore.

Fortunata was only ten years old. Maria convinced Fortunata to move to the town of Porticello to live with the Tarantinos, her uncle and aunt, because she claimed Fortunata would grow up in a better environment.

Maria decided to speak with her cousins Lucrezia and Santo Tarantino. Lucrezia, who was never married, was a teacher of design and embroidery.

Santo, the brother, was a handsome, young, elegant, intelligent bachelor. He was the captain of a large passenger ship which traveled from Palermo and Naples to New York.

He led the beautiful life of a sea-faring Don Giovanni, with a different beautiful woman in every port, returning home every three months.

When Lucrezia heard all that Maria had said and the conditions set down by her husband, she said to her, "You have done the right thing, bringing your daughter to me. I am alone, and my brother only returns home every three months. He has only a few days before leaving once again. Therefore, having a child with me would bring me a lot of pleasure."

Lucrezia continued, "I will teach Fortunata the same skills that I already teach my students. I also have a little monkey named Bella, whom Fortunata can play with whenever she wants. Every Sunday, I will go to church and bring Fortunata to help her establish friendships with other children of the same age."

Captain Santo Tarantino

Maria felt very sad upon leaving her daughter, but she consoled herself because she knew her daughter was well cared for.

She returned to San Nicola and continued to live her usual life.

Maria thought often of her daughter when she was alone. It was her husband's fault that her daughter would grow up far from her mother.

She was sad, and she cried, but there was nothing she could do about it except to pray and see her once a week. But she was happy every week when she saw and stayed with her daughter.

CHAPTER 6

As the years went by, Fortunata developed into a beautiful young woman. Back in San Nicola, all the children of Don Nino grew up as well.

Don Nino thought about what his father taught him about not following in the path of the Mafia, being strong and courageous, helping those in need, making the right decisions, and living a calm life without problems.

After considering all this, he said, "I believe that I have done well deciding to have Salvatore marry Fortunata."

Marietta, Don Nino's eldest daughter, was now married and living in Trabia, the town neighboring San Nicola. Bastiano, however, had chosen the life of a mafioso.

Don Nino went to Bastiano and gave him an ultimatum. He said, "Leave the Mafia and return to a normal life by helping me with my businesses, or renounce this family and be dead to me from now on.

If you do not change, I never want to see or talk to you again."

Bastiano replied, "I love you dearly, Papa, but I am not like the others who slavishly obey you, doing everything you say and want. For me, it is wrong. I want to live my life the way that I want, even if you do not agree."

Disappointed and furious, Don Nino replied to his son, "Get out of this house and never return!"

Bastiano left and looked for a place to stay and continue living his life.

Father and Sons

Bastiano was the leader of the young mafiosi. Five young men, known as the Picciotti, worked for him.

The older men were known as Mafia or the 'friends of the friends.'

Bastiano was strong, courageous, and smart. He did not do harm to anyone and even tried to help those in need.

The people trusted and respected him.

Bastiano was not angry with his father.

When he had the chance to see the rest of the family, including Maria, he greeted them, and they spoke without his father knowing about it.

Salvatrice and Francesca studied. Salvatore enlisted in the Italian Navy with the intention of becoming an officer. He served on a ship named Carcia Tarpotiniera.

From a fleet of twenty ships, Salvatore was chosen as the leader of an escort for the king of Italy, Umberto of Savoy, and his son on a trip from Tripoli to Taranto.

This was a great honor for Salvatore; he continued the service and enjoyed his work.

Salvatrice and Francesca studied. Salvatore enlisted in the Italian Navy with the intention of becoming an officer. He served on a ship named Carcia Tarpotiniera.

From a fleet of twenty ships, Salvatore was chosen as the leader of an escort for the king of Italy, Umberto of Savoy, and his son on a trip from Tripoli to Taranto.

This was a great honor for Salvatore; he continued the service and enjoyed his work.

After three years in the Navy, Salvatore returned home. Everyone was satisfied to see him and proud that he was chosen for this honor. They celebrated his return by holding a beautiful party.

Bastiano & Picciotti

Salvatore LoBuono in Uniform

Salvatore was glad to be back home with his family, especially his father, whom he helped with the fieldwork.

Everything was going well upon Salvatore's return until one day, his father, Don Nino, stated that Salvatore was to marry Fortunata.

Surprised and disappointed, Salvatore responded, "Papa, you did not even give me time to enjoy my return home before revealing this news to me. I love you very much and have always obeyed your wishes until now, but what you are now proposing to me is impossible."

He continued, "Fortunata and I were raised together; I love her like a sister. I do not think what you are suggesting will succeed. And besides, I have not seen Fortunata for a long time, and you do not know how she will react to this news. You have made a mistake in making this decision."

Don Nino responded, "I will make her an offer she cannot refuse."

Salvatore asked, "And what is your proposal?"

Don Nino replied, "Do not think about it, my son. This is my work and my decision. You need to obey, like the rest of the family. I will think of everything and inform you of the results in a few weeks."

Several days later, Don Nino spoke with his wife and told her, "Maria, the time has come for you to speak with your daughter."

He continued, "Give her the news that Salvatore has returned and wants to see her. I want them to see each other again, and then we will decide when they should get married."

Maria answered, "Okay. I will speak with my daughter, but I cannot promise she will accept your proposal. Tomorrow, I will take the train to Porticello. When I return, I will let you know my daughter's response."

The following day, when she arrived at the village where Fortunata was living, she was so happy to see her daughter again, kissing and embracing her.

Fortunata looked at her mother and said, "Mamma, you look sad. Is anything wrong? Do you feel sick?"

She continued, "You do not look like the other times when you came here to visit me. Talk to me, Mamma, and tell me what is wrong."

Maria looked at her daughter, not knowing how to break the news to her. But she knew she needed to be courageous and tell Fortunata what Don Nino had decided.

"Fortunata, my darling daughter, I love you very much. I see you are happy. I have made many sacrifices for your well-being and sent you away from me because I felt it would be better for you," Maria said.

"It breaks my heart to give you this news. I miss you very much and want to be near you, but destiny has separated us. Perhaps it is my fault. I have not thought about what could happen in the future."

Maria continued, "When I got married, I only thought about your future. Now, I am not certain if I did right or wrong. Sometimes, I believe it would have been better if we had gone to live with my sister in America."

Fortunata was upset upon hearing her mother speak in this fashion.

Fortunata & Mother Maria

Fortunata's Father Carmelo Rizzo

She said, "Mamma, I love and miss you very much. I do not like to see you in this state. You are too worried."

Maria still looked concerned. Fortunata said, "Please tell me what is in your head causing you to feel this way. Speak with me. Do not hide anything from me. I am your daughter, and you can speak frankly with me."

Maria replied, "Okay, but I do not think you will want to hear what I am going to say. My husband has insisted I inform you that he has made a decision. His son Salvatore, who has just returned home after a three-year absence, is to become your husband."

Fortunata, completely upset, responded, "Your husband is crazy. He cannot make me marry Salvatore! I love him like a brother, not like a lover. Besides, I met a boy in church, and he is the one I am in love with."

She continued, "Return home now and tell your husband I will never accept his crazy decision! I am sorry for you, Mamma, but I hope you can understand me."

They said goodbye to one another, and Maria returned to San Nicola.

That evening, at dinnertime, when Don Nino returned home, he asked her, "Eh beh? What did your daughter say?"

Maria did know how to respond. She hesitated momentarily and replied, "Nino, I am sorry to tell you what my daughter said. She told me that she loves another boy and will never accept the idea of marrying Salvatore because she loves him like a brother."

Furious and shocked, Don Nino slammed his fist on the table and screamed. "This is not possible. She cannot refuse me!"

He continued, "I want you to return to your daughter tomorrow and tell her that if she does not marry my son, I will no longer allow you to handle the money I earn from my businesses. You tell her that if my son should marry someone else, I will remove you from any connection with managing my money and instead put my son's future spouse in charge of everything."

Disgusted and worried, Maria never imagined that her husband would treat her this way.

She resented that she had married him and was very confused because she did not know what to do.

She did not want to let her sister in America know what was happening and felt guilty that she had never gone to the US with her daughter.

Life would have been different. Instead, she decided to get married, and now that she had discovered her husband's true nature, she realized that whatever he decided, not only she but everyone in the family needed to obey.

She did not like this but understood that her husband's word was law around here. Therefore, she decided to visit her daughter once again.

When she arrived, Fortunata realized there would be a problem and immediately asked, "What happened now?" Fortunata said.

"Tell me! Do not hide anything from me! I want to know everything! I am no longer a little girl, and I do not want to see you suffer."

Maria hugged her daughter, and as she cried, she responded, "My daughter. If I could go back in time, I would say that instead of marrying Don Nino, I would have preferred to go with you to my sister in America."

"Why do you say this, mamma?" Fortunata asked her.

"Because my husband controls everyone, and like everybody else, I must obey. Also, he punishes those who do not do what he wants."

Maria continued, "He has made me an offer. If you do not marry Salvatore, he will remove me from managing his monetary affairs and replace me in this position with whomever eventually marries Salvatore."

"Can you imagine how he treats me? My future will be ruined, and so will yours. Fortunata, my daughter, I am so sorry. I do not wish to make you suffer because of my mistakes. I recommend that you marry whomever you want and wish that you will be happy. If I must suffer, it is because God wants it that way, and I will accept whatever destiny has in store for me."

Fortunata responded, "Mamma, listen to me very carefully. I do not want you to suffer for me. Return to your husband and tell him I want a couple of months to think about it and get to know Salvatore better. I will see you in a few weeks. I will speak with Salvatore, and then we shall decide what to do. Go, Mamma, and do not be sad. Everything is going to be all right."

Maria returned to San Nicola and reported everything to her husband.

He was not satisfied, but he told his wife that he would grant Fortunata the time she requested to decide, and then they would speak about it.

CHAPTER 7

For a few days, everything proceeded normally until Don Nino found the opportunity to speak with his son Salvatore.

"Listen to me, my son. Fortunata will come to San Nicola once a week. I will arrange everything so that she remains alone."

Don Nino continued, "You will ascend the stairs, and upon entering the room, you will close the door behind you. Even if the two of you do nothing on this day, you will still need to get married. Because if you do not get married, it will be a disgrace for her."

In shock at what his father is proposing, Salvatore tells Don Nino, "Papa, how could you propose such a thing to me! I do not want to do anything bad to Fortunata. I do not like what you are telling me. I am not happy with what you are suggesting for me to do."

"However, I know I must obey you and cannot say no. You need to decide and do everything for all of us, and no one can change your mind. Therefore, I will do what you want," Salvatore reluctantly told him.

One week later, on a Saturday, Fortunata went to San Nicola. Everyone welcomed her with great pleasure. She greeted Salvatore, whom she had not seen for three years.

They began to speak to each other. Meanwhile, supper was ready, and everyone sat down to eat.

Fortunata sat next to Salvatore.

With tears in her eyes, Maria looked at her daughter and thought of the sacrifice that her daughter would make on her behalf.

They began to eat, each person directing their comments toward Fortunata, saying, "How beautiful you look! How well-dressed you are! Black and white suits you well. Even your hairstyle is pretty."

Fortunata thanked everyone for the warm welcome and the positive compliments.

When they finished eating, Fortunata offered to clean the kitchen, stating, "I need to get ready to go so that I don't miss the return train to Porticello."

Don Nino replied, "Fortunata, do not make jokes regarding cleaning the kitchen; you are my guest and thus do not need to do any work here."

"As for the train," he said, "It is already nine in the evening, and I will not permit you to travel at this late hour."

Don Nino continued, "There are enough bedrooms for you to spend the night with us. Tomorrow, you will feel more relaxed, and in the meantime, you will be able to go and spend some time with Salvatore."

Fortunata, looking at her mother, responded, "Okay. I will leave tomorrow. Thank you for the hospitality you have given me."

They kept speaking to each other until it was time to sleep.

Everyone said good night and then went to bed. The next day, the family sat down for breakfast around nine o'clock.

After everyone finished eating and left, Fortunata remained alone. For Fortunata, that particular Sunday was very relaxing and tranquil.

Fortunata Rizzo

She began to prepare herself to go and take the train. In the meantime, she noticed dust on the furniture and tried to clean it.

She felt good doing something before going away. When she finished, she arranged the doors and windows. When she went towards the exit, suddenly, she heard the sound of heavy footsteps on the stairs, which led to her room.

The steps grew increasingly louder and louder.

Fortunata asked, "Who is it? Who is there?"

Nobody replied. Meanwhile, the footsteps were growing increasingly nearer and louder.

Fortunata continued asking, "Who is it? Why don't you answer me?"

Fortunata suspected that it was someone who wanted to do her harm. Therefore, she approached the balcony, thinking that if she needed to, she could scream, and someone would come to her aid.

Fortunata did not realize it, but only Salvatore was ascending the stairwell.

He purposefully made noise to alert Fortunata about his presence so that she might lock the door before he arrived in her room.

Fortunata thought that she would not be able to lock the door in time, so it would be better to approach the balcony.

Salvatore arrived, entered, and then locked the door. Fortunata understood what he wanted to do and suddenly jumped off the balcony.

Miraculously, she landed unharmed on her feet.

However, she suffered from an extreme case of shock and was unable to move.

Someone saw her and immediately ran to her aid. Seeing that Fortunata had leaped from the balcony, Salvatore ran downstairs to see if she had suffered any harm.

A furious Fortunata asked, "Why did you do this? What did you have in mind when you came to my room like this?"

Salvatore responded, "Fortunata, please forgive me. I did not want to do this. It was my father who ordered me to come here because he did not want you to refuse to marry me.

Salvatore continued, "Believe me, I love you very much. Because of this, I purposely made a loud noise with my shoes when I was going up the stairs. I hoped that you would lock the door in time. Instead, you had the idea of jumping off the balcony.

Fortunata, you could have died. Why did you do it!"

Fortunata replied, "It was an instinct. I did not think that there was enough time to lock the door. Plus, I did not know that it was you; I thought somebody was coming to hurt me."

She continued, "When I saw that you closed and locked the door behind you, I knew what you were going to do. Your father might control you, but he does not control me."

"Never in this world will he accomplish the goal he sent you here for. Salvatore, if I am to marry you, tell your father not to ever do again what he tried to do here today, because I want to get married wearing a white dress in church. I do not want to disappoint my mother."

"Do you understand?"

Salvatore responded, "I promise you that what my father ordered me to do will never happen again. What he wanted was crazy and absurd. I never wanted to do this."

"Fortunata, take all the time you need, and when you are ready, we will decide the date and the month when we should get married. I love you very much, even if you do not love me, I will make you incredibly happy."

Chapter 8

Some time passed. After four months, Salvatore and Fortunata were married in a church, exactly as Fortunata had wanted.

Everything went perfectly, and Don Nino arranged a beautiful wedding party for them.

Don Nino also prepared a place for them to live, with furniture and everything else they needed.

He was happy that his son had married Fortunata. He did everything possible to make them feel welcome and comfortable, as did his wife.

Don Nino was satisfied that he had reached the goal which he had set for himself.

Salvatore did everything to make Fortunata happy, and they were both content.

They were living a normal life, and even Fortunata's mother was happy because she had her daughter nearby.

Salvatore and other men usually helped his father in the fields.

Salvatrice and Francesca, after Marietta, also got married. Don Nino provided a generous dowry to the three girls and gave each one of them her own house.

Bastiano did not want to listen to his father or obey him, instead choosing to take the path of the Mafia.

Don Nino was unhappy that his son did not listen to his counsel and was not pleased with what he was doing.

Fortunata & Salvatore Wedding

Antonino LoBuono – Don Nino and Maria's son

Because Bastiano refused to follow his father's advice, Don Nino did not want his son to continue living in the family home and decided he would never see or speak to him again.

When Don Nino married his third wife, Maria D'Aquisto, he had a son whom he named Antonino after himself. Antonino was, therefore, the brother of Salvatore through his father and brother to Fortunata through her mother.

When Antonino turned twenty during the Second World War, Don Nino became worried about what would happen to his son.

Thanks to his connections, Don Nino sent his son to Rome to hide him in St. Peter's Church, where he remained for two and a half years.

While hiding there, he met a young woman who would sing Ave Maria during Mass every Sunday.

Her name was Vincenza. They fell in love and were married within a few months in the same church.

At the end of the war, they returned to Sicily. His father did not have the time to prepare a proper place for them to live, so he could only offer them a single room.

Vincenza was a beautiful girl with long, wavy blonde hair, but she had one serious issue. She was extremely jealous of Fortunata, who had a house provided with expensive furniture.

Fortunata tried to be helpful to her, even offering help if necessary.

After two years of marriage, Fortunata was pregnant with her first child.

The husband and wife were happy with their life together. After nine months, Fortunata gave birth to a baby girl whom she named Mariella.

Ariana, Fortunata & Mariella

Fortunata's mother was also quite pleased that she had now become a grandmother.

When the time came for the baptism, Fortunata wanted her mother to serve as godmother to the newborn.

Life continued as normal.

After two years had passed, Fortunata gave birth to another baby whom she wanted to name after her father, Carmelo.

But when she saw the baby, she realized it was a beautiful second baby girl. She then decided the name would not work, so they came up with Ariana.

As the days passed, Fortunata was very content with her life. Her husband was so helpful with the kids, and she never felt alone or unhappy.

During the day, Salvatore labored with his father in the fields. In the evening, he would come home, relax, and play with his daughters while his wife prepared supper.

Some years passed. Mariella turned four, and Ariana was now two. The two sisters got along well and often played together. Life for the family was good.

One day, when Don Nino and his son Salvatore were working in the field, his other son Antonino came to speak with his father.

Antonino said, "Papa, since my wife and I have been here, she has felt unhappy. I have decided to leave Sicily for her sake."

He continued, "I do not want to work with you and Salvatore in the fields. My dream is to become a detective. I am coming to you because I would like your blessing to allow me to follow my dream."

Don Nino replied, "If this is what you really want and it will make you happy, you have my blessing. However, can you agree to see me at least once a year?"

Antonino replied, "Yes, Papa, and thank you."

Antonino then went to his wife to tell her the great news.

He said, "My father has given me his blessing to follow my dream. We will leave as soon as possible. Please tell me, do you have any idea of where you would like to live?"

She replied, "Yes. I would like to live in the beautiful city of Vercelli."

A couple of days passed, and they set out on their new adventure.

Within one year in Vercelli, Antonino had become a detective, or as he calls it, Finanziere.

They were blessed with a beautiful baby boy named Franco during this time.

Antonino kept his promise to his father and visited Sicily once a year.

CHAPTER 9

Winter was near, and things were going well until one day, everything suddenly changed.

The fickle hand of fate was waiting to disrupt the tranquility in the family's life.

Don Nino and Salvatore were in the fields observing the olive trees, which were full of olives.

Both father and son were happy because the crop was doing well and would yield the family some much-needed money.

While they were speaking, there was a noise; they saw two carabinieri who were busy filling two large chests with olives.

Don Nino approached them, "Buon giorno. Who gave you permission to enter my property?"

Salvatore watched his father and prepared himself for whatever might happen.

The two young carabinieri were armed with both machine guns and pistols.

The two men approached Don Nino with arrogance and self-assurance.

Don Nino yelled at the two men, "How dare you come on my property and steal my olives! If you had only asked, I would have given you what you wanted, but you must pay for what you have taken or leave the olives here and get off my land now!"

They did not reply to him.

He waited, but they still refused to answer.

Finally, the two arrogant carabinieri said, "We do not pay, and we will take the baskets of olives. You cannot do anything about it!"

The insolence of their words and the arrogance of their black and white pipe uniforms aroused a tremendous fury in Don Nino's breast.

Salvatore looked at his father and wanted to help him. Don Nino raised his hand to stop his son. He was thinking that he would never allow Salvatore to be arrested.

In the meantime, the two carabinieri were trying to leave. Don Nino stopped them and said: "You may go. But you must leave the olives you were stealing from me here."

The two young men started to laugh. One approached Don Nino and pushed him with the intent that he should fall.

Don Nino, however, did not go down. His pride would not allow anyone to knock him off his feet.

The other carabinieri saw that Nino would not fall, so he furiously charged at Don Nino to push him down.

Salvatore knew he would never allow these men to harm his father or rob him and his family.

He moved towards the carabinieri, who did not see him coming. He hit one of the men with his forearm, knocking him to the ground.

Salvatore said, "You do not push my father. If you have something to say, say it to me!"

The other carabinieri was shocked to see what Salvatore had done. He launched his body against Salvatore and attempted to launch him into a very deep burrone (ravine).

When Salvatore saw the infuriated carabinieri running towards him, he quickly moved away from his opponent, who then fell into the ravine and died immediately.

Meanwhile, the other carabinieri raised himself off the floor and approached Salvatore.

He had seen everything and attempted to grab Salvatore by the jacket to push him into the ravine.

Salvatore was stronger than his enemy and seized the carabiniere's uniform, from which a button fell to the ground.

The carabinieri was the one who fell into the ravine instead of Salvatore.

Fortunately for the carabinieri, he grabbed the enormous roots of an olive tree growing nearby to save his life.

The frightened man then desperately cried out, "Help me! Help me!"

Hearing the carabinieri's plea for help, Salvatore drew closer to the fallen man, looked him in the eyes, and said, "Yell. Yell for help as much as you want, but no one can hear you here. No one will help you."

He continued, "This will be a lesson to you not to steal from someone's property and not be rude to others just because you are wearing a policeman's uniform."

Don Nino, who had seen everything, called to his son, yelling, "Run, run away, my son. Hide in the mountains. I will send you help. Go. Run. May God help you!"

Salvatore escaped and headed towards the mountains. Don Nino headed towards the exit to go home, but he was stopped by another carabinieri who asked him if he had seen two other carabinieri who had passed that way.

Don Nino, thinking quickly, responded that he had not seen either man on his property and resumed his march home.

Meanwhile, the man holding on to the roots of the olive tree continued to scream louder and louder for help so that someone might hear his cries and come to his aid.

Eventually, four of his comrades, who had been making their daily rounds in the area, heard his cries for help and extracted him from the olive branch.

The comrades soon noticed the dead body of the other carabinieri lying at the bottom of the ravine.

They asked the surviving officer what had happened to him and his unfortunate partner.

He explained to them what had happened but distorted the events to make it seem as if it was Don Nino and his son who were responsible for the violence that ensued.

When the carabinieri returned to the barracks, a writ of arrest was issued for both Don Nino and his son Salvatore.

In the meantime, after Don Nino returned home, the first thing he did was to contact some powerful people he had helped in the past.

He requested their help after explaining what had transpired with the two carabinieri.

He asked for two bodyguards for his son. Within hours, Salvatore found himself under the protection of two bodyguards in case he needed help.

Don Nino thanked them and said, "I will let you know when you can come to my house so we can speak further."

After his father told him to run away to the mountains, Salvatore knew exactly where to go. The grotto in which he hid was a long cave that terminated in a mass of boulders that nearly reached the top of the cave.

When Salvatore and Bastiano were children, they used to go to the fields with their father and discovered this same cave, which was close to the vineyards and olive fields.

They squeezed past the rocks in the cave and found that it led to a passage that ended in an opening on the other side of the mountain.

Salvatore felt very comfortable inside the cave.

In the afternoon, he saw two tall, strong men arrive at the cave. He asked them who they were and what they wanted.

They, in turn, replied, "We are here to help you. We will make sure that nothing happens to you."

Then, they continued, "Your father sent us here, and we will follow the orders we were given. Therefore, please be calm and enjoy the company."

In the meantime, the Maresciallo of the Trabia Carabiniere issued a proclamation stating that the man on the run must surrender within 12 hours or his entire family would be arrested.

Two days later, the carabinieri arrived at Don Nino's house and stated that they intended to arrest Don Nino and Salvatore.

Don Nino did not resist, telling them, "You can arrest me but not my son because he is not here, and I do not know where he is. Therefore, do your duty, and we will see what happens afterward."

The carabinieri proceeded to handcuff Don Nino, read him his rights under the law, and then took him to the police barracks.

Before leaving, the carabinieri turned to Fortunata and said to her, "We will be returning for your husband."

After several days, Salvatore's brother Bastiano heard about what had transpired with his father and brother.

He did not hesitate to do what was necessary to help his family.

For the first time in many years, he spoke to Salvatore about the reality of life in Sicily.

He knew where Salvatore was hiding, and he would find him.

Bastiano arrived at the cave and found Salvatore just as he had expected he would. The two brothers embraced each other.

Bastiano said to Salvatore, "My dear brother, no one admires your good qualities more than I. I love you very much and hope you will allow me to help you and Father get out of the mess you are both in now."

Salvatore responded, "I also love you very much. You know it was not my fault that you were thrown out of the house. You know it was our father's fault. Whatever he says must be done, and he punishes anyone who does not listen to him."

Salvatore continued, "You know that he forced me to marry Fortunata. I loved her like a sister, not like a wife. Since we have been married, we have two young girls. And you? Are you now married, or are you still a bachelor?"

"Bastiano, it has been an immense pleasure to see you, and I appreciate your offer of help very much. If you want to help us, that is fine with me. But I want you to be careful because I do not want anything to happen to you on my account."

Bastiano looked at his brother and said, "Do you recall when you were ten years old, and I was eight, and we discovered this cave? Who would ever have guessed that after so many years, we would return to that place again for any reason? Therefore, it is great pleasure that you allow me to help you."

"Tomorrow, I will return with my men, and we will bring you all the items that you need. I will leave you three men who will watch over you at night so you can sleep calmly, knowing that people are watching out in case you need to escape."

Bastiano continued, "If I forget anything, let me know, and I will make a trip back. I want to make sure that you are comfortable."

Salvatore responded, "Do not take too many risks; otherwise, someone might see you and become suspicious of what you are doing here."

Bastiano replied, "Salvatore, the carabinieri knows that Papa threw me out of the house, and therefore, we have not spoken for a long time. They will not think that I will help both of you. And in response to your first question, no, I am not married. I will say goodbye for now, and we will see each other tomorrow."

The next day, at 3:30 a.m., Bastiano, accompanied by some of his men, went back to see his brother.

They brought a mattress for sleeping, blankets for cover, a lamp to provide light during the night, water, wine, bread, fruit, and more.

Salvatore thanked his brother for everything he had brought him, saying, "Bastiano, why did you do all of this for me? You know that our father would not be satisfied or content with this. What would happen if he ever found out?"

Bastiano responded, "Salvatore, it is not important to me if he finds out or not. The reason for helping you is that I love you very much. You are my brother. And even if Papa does not like it, I will also help him even if he never speaks to me again!"

Salvatore replied, "Papa sent me two bodyguards to protect me. I thank you and hope to see and hear from you again."

"Certainly, we will meet again," said Bastiano, "and with these three other men, you will be safe in case the carabinieri should come here. They are under orders to shoot to give you the chance to escape with the bodyguards. I am not saying that this will happen, but it is better to be safe in case something bad should occur. Now I am leaving. The next time I come here, I will let you know about what is happening. Goodbye for now."

They embraced, and Bastiano left.

CHAPTER 10

Don Nino spoke to his lawyer, Mormino, who paid the bond. Mormino told Don Nino, "We must wait until the court date."

Salvatore, the son of Don Nino, the leader of the youth of San Nicola, the most respected and powerful, the one acknowledged as the strongest and most fearless man, a true Sicilian, the one who teaches his kids to be strong, and honest to be proud and fear no one.

As he lay on the mattress, Salvatore wondered, 'Am I ever going to be like my father?'

That night, he could not sleep.

He thought the gold sun was glorious early in the morning, and the smell of lemon and olive trees filled the air.

The bodyguard asked Salvatore why he had not slept. "You must rest. We will watch over you, and with us, nothing will happen to you. Be calm and tranquil, at least if you want to move from here and go to a different place."

"No," Salvatore responded, "I follow my father's orders. I must wait here until my father is released."

The morning air was clear and crisp. Close to Salvatore, a prickly pear on the ground was cold and sweet.

Salvatore picked up two of them to eat and refresh his mouth. In a few hours, the sun's heat would dry the pears into shriveled cotton balls.

In the meantime, back in San Nicola, Don Nino received a visit from a friend. He led his friend across the open ground to the main house.

Armed men were patrolling near the wall. The house was close to the sea, a small dock straight towards the faraway coast.

A large, slick motorboat with Italian and Sicilian flags was at the dock.

Two other friends who worked for Don Nino were inside the house. He asked them to bring a bowl of fruit, cheese, and wine.

The terrace looked over the blue Mediterranean Sea, which seemed to part in the middle when heated by a shaft of morning sunlight.

A fishing boat with a bright blue and red sail buffeted on the horizon ball, skipping over the water.

There was a small table on the terrace covered with a dark blue cloth, and the guests sat around it. A pot of espresso and a bottle of red wine were on the table for the guests to enjoy.

Don Nino said, "As you wish, have an espresso or a glass of wine. This is my own wine. I would like your opinion of it."

They responded, "We want a glass of wine." They started to drink, and they liked it very much.

They complimented the wine and said, "From now on, we will do business with you. Of course, we would like to buy wine, oil, and all kinds of fruit."

Don Nino thanked his friends, responding, "With great pleasure. And I also want to say thank you to the two bodyguards who are helping my son."

His friend asked, "How are things going? Is there anything new? How is your son? We feel and understand how you feel. You are extremely attached to, and proud of, your son."

Don Nino responded, "It is true. My son obeys my every word. He has never said a harsh word to me. He is a loving, dutiful son. On his first day as an outlaw, he looked down from the mountain, thinking about his father and wife, and I wish I could do more."

Don Nino said, "The carabinieri came here, and I said it is okay for me but not for my son. I spent only one night in jail. My lawyer did what was necessary to free me from prison. Now, we must await our day in court."

"As you have seen, my house is surrounded by carabiniere. The Marshall of Trabia sends a patrol every night into the street. His godson beefed up the patrol to one hundred men every night." Don Nino continued, "They are alert, guarding the entirety of my house. They think that my son will come here and speak with me. They are wasting their time because my son will never come here. Dear friends, my house will always be open to you. Anytime."

The friends replied, "The same is true for us. And if you need us, we will always be ready to help you. Now we need to leave, and we will see you in a few days."

They said their goodbyes, and Don Nino's friends left to go on their way.

As the day passed, Salvatore seemed to retire more into his private world.

Weeks went by as he waited for his brother or father to send a messenger about how things were going in San Nicola.

One morning, he wandered deep into the mountain by himself, thinking about what was going to happen and whether he was going to see his family again, especially his father. The bodyguards watched every move he made.

As the day became night, Salvatore lay on top of the mattress and felt the presence of his family and their love.

This made him strong enough to pass the time.

In the meantime, Fortunata was also thinking about him.

At the same moment, they were both sad because they could feel each other's presence and love and were close.

Fortunata said, "Jesus, help my husband. Good night, my love."

Salvatore looked at the sky stitched with stars, said, "Good night, my love," and then went to sleep.

As he slept, he dreamed of his wife cooking, arranging a hot bath, and preparing a soft bed in his room, but more importantly, his wife's white skin.

He missed hugging her and making love.

Salvatore relished the freshness of late spring, the beauty of the mountain on the horizon, and the knowledge that three men were in the underbrush, watching the road with guns.

After a couple of days, his godfather Giuseppe visited him in the night, sent by Don Nino.

Salvatore was pleased to see and talk with him.

He explained his situation, and Giuseppe listened to him without words or change of expression.

Giuseppe said, "Salvatore, you were always a fine, brave young man with a good heart, sincere, generous, and sympathetic. I will do anything that your father asks me. Count on my helping in this and all other things."

Giuseppe continued, "Your father is immensely proud to have a son like you, and so am I. Do not worry because everything will be resolved for the best, and it will seem like a bad dream for you. When you wake up, it will be better."

Now I must go, but we will see each other in a few days, and I will tell you how things are going.

Giuseppe embraced Salvatore and said, "This is it for now. Be well, and God bless you."

The sea shined in the golden rays of the Sicilian noontime sun.

Veins of red light struck the earth as if reflecting the bloodshed on Sicily's soil for countless centuries. After several days, Giuseppe went to visit Don Nino.

Giuseppe said, "Salvatore is well, but he is always sad because he misses his wife and children."

He continued, "Compare, we need to do something to help Salvatore see his wife."

Don Nino responded, "Truly, I have an idea, but we must be alert because, as you know, my house is surrounded by the carabinieri."

Giuseppe said, "We should try to send Fortunata to church alone. Sunday after mass, I will have Fortunata leave through the back of the church and take her back to my house."

He continued, "When it gets late in the night, around three in the morning, I will take her to Salvatore, and thus, they will have the chance to spend some time together."

"Very good, Compare," responded Don Nino.

"I will speak with Fortunata, who will be incredibly pleased with the opportunity to see her husband again.

We will agree to arrange things this way." They said goodbye to each other, and Giuseppe left.

Chapter 11

As Sunday approached two days later, Fortunata prepared to go to church.

When she arrived at church, she saw her husband's godfather, Giuseppe, and noticed he was making a signal to get her attention.

After mass, they met and left together at the back of the church.

Giuseppe was alert and looked everywhere to see if anybody might have seen Fortunata leaving the building or could have followed them.

When Giuseppe was certain that no one had seen them leave or followed behind them, he took Fortunata back to his house with him.

Three in the morning came, and it was very dark, but Giuseppe and Fortunata parted to see Salvatore.

When Fortunata arrived, Salvatore could not believe his eyes. He was so surprised to see his wife but nevertheless incredibly happy.

He hugged his wife, and they kissed. Then he said, "What have you done? It is very risky to come here to see me. I do not want anything to happen to you. How are the children?"

Fortunata assured her husband, "Be calm; it is okay. Your godfather helped me come here, and he has done a very good job making sure that nobody saw us leave. I have not stopped worrying about you. I worry about how you are eating, whether you are feeling well or cold out here. Tell me what you do for food."

Salvatore replied, "It will be a surprise for you. I will tell you, but please, I ask you not to say anything to my father."

Salvatore continued, "My brother Bastiano has brought me everything that I have needed, including food."

"He left behind three men who guard the street and have orders to shoot anyone who approaches here where I am. Also, he tells me what is happening in the city."

Fortunata responded, "You are right. I am really surprised but incredibly happy at the same time. I would never have imagined that this would have happened after so much time. If you see him again, thank him for me."

"Your godfather is waiting outside for you. Please ask him if we can have some privacy and give him my greetings."

"Your father was incarcerated for only one night since his lawyer came to free him the next day. But he is very worried about you and has said he will do everything in his power to help you."

Fortunata continued, "He cannot go anywhere because the house is surrounded by carabinieri. One of them said to me that they would arrest you in a short time. I replied to him and stared at his face. Tell me, how would you feel in this situation?"

Salvatore replied, "I do not like it at all. I want to return home to be with you and the children. I would never have imagined such a thing happening to me and my father."

Fortunata caressed him and said, "You must be strong and have patience, courage, and faith in God, and everything will work itself out. And for you, this will seem like a bad dream that you and I will tell each other with a smile."

"Now, my love, I must leave you. I will try to come here another time. I will always be with you in my thoughts. I love you very much, my dear."

They kissed each other, and she left.

At Easter time in Sicily, it has always been a tradition for the entire family to get together and attend church.

Salvatore felt sad because he wanted to be with his family for the Easter holiday.

Four days before Easter, as he was speaking to his brother, he said, "What must I do to go to San Nicola and go at least to church? Thus, I could see my wife and children?"

Bastiano replied, "I have an idea, but it will be very risky for you. I will try my best, and tomorrow I will tell you what we can do."

When Bastiano returned the next day, he told Salvatore, "I have a surprise for you."

Salvatore looked at him and said, "Tell me about this surprise."

"Here is a bag full of what you need to change yourself," Bastiano said.

Salvatore opened the bag and, turning towards Bastiano, said, "But these are women's things," he began to smile.

Bastiano smiled and said, "Yes, you are right; it is a woman's outfit, a wig, a jacket, and a scarf."

"If you are going to return to the village, you must dress as a woman. You must be aware that we will always be near you and around you. You will need to enter through the back of the church, and when you see your wife, you will need to sit beside her. We will think of the rest."

Salvatore thanked his brother and asked him, "Do you think I will be able to get to the church?"

"Certainly," said Bastiano, "I guarantee it. Now for tonight, just relax, and we will come for you tomorrow."

The next day, Bastiano and his men came to fetch Salvatore.

Bastiano looked at his brother and said, "You have done a wonderful job dressing yourself like a woman. You really do make for such a beautiful-looking lady!"

Finally, after eight months of hiding, Salvatore, accompanied by his bodyguards, Bastiano, and Bastiano's men, could leave the mountains to see his wife and children.

Two men were walking twenty paces ahead of him.

Two other men walked on the other side of him, and more men were walking behind him.

If Salvatore were to be stopped by the carabinieri to arrest him, they would be his target for these men. The men were prepared to shoot without mercy.

When Salvatore and his two bodyguards entered the church from the back, everybody was alert to what was happening when they saw Salvatore standing close to his wife.

For a moment, Salvatore felt so peaceful that he enjoyed smelling the perfume of exotic subtropical flowers on the altar.

Fortunata was already aware that Salvatore would be dressed like a woman, and she did everything she could to ensure that Salvatore would be able to sit beside her.

Even if they could not physically touch each other, she was content with him just being near her.

The children did not say anything because they did not know their father was there.

Bastiano, his men, and the friends of the friends, all of whom accompanied Salvatore, covered every area of the church, both inside and outside.

They were all on the lookout to ensure that nothing bad would happen to Salvatore.

If they noticed a problem with the carabinieri, they were ready to shoot to protect Salvatore.

Since Salvatore was dressed as a woman in order not to be recognized, the police counted on the deep tie of the family to bring the outlaw sneaking down from the mountain to visit his loved ones.

On the day before Easter, two carabinieri entered Don Nino's house. They were there to warn him that if his son Salvatore should descend from the mountain in the direction of San Nicola to visit his family, the carabinieri, they would make sure to arrest him, and he would not be able to leave for many years.

Salvatore, with the aid of his godfather Giuseppe, advised his father that he was going down to visit his family with the bodyguard and many men who were friends of friends and would disguise himself as a woman.

When Don Nino heard this, he started to prepare a big feast to celebrate the Easter holiday.

On Sunday morning, all the family except Don Nino went to morning mass because the carabinieri surrounded his house and was all over town.

Nobody suspected that Salvatore was dressed as a woman in church with his family.

When mass concluded, one of the bodyguards approached Salvatore.

"The marshal of Palermo ordered twenty carabinieri, and at this time, they are inside and outside your house because they thought you might come home to visit your family," the bodyguard said.

He continued, "Your father will deal with the carabiniere. You will not return home. We need to return to the mountain before anyone suspects anything."

"Therefore, Salvatore, it is time to say goodbye to your wife and children. We must go now before they see you!"

Salvatore kissed his wife and children and said to his wife, "Do not worry. Go back home and enjoy the rest of this holiday with the kids. Say hello to my father. I will be okay."

He then left and returned with the bodyguards and the men, who were heavily armed and ready to shoot if needed, to the mountain.

Salvatore was incredibly lucky that nobody recognized him.

He thanked his brother for the idea and for helping him go to the village to be with his family in church on the holy day of Easter.

Father and Sons

CHAPTER 12

Outside, Sicily's May sun was hot as usual, but the mountain breeze cooled the air.

Salvatore was thinking about when he would be free to return home to his family.

Fortunata was also sad and thought about making a surprise visit to her husband.

With Salvatore's godfather's help, she visited her husband. Salvatore, seeing his wife, was incredibly pleased.

He hugged and kissed his wife and then said, "Fortunata, it gives me immense pleasure to see you, but you need to make sure that nobody sees you or follows you. I do not want anything to happen to you. With whom did you come here?"

Fortunata replied, "I came here with your godfather. I do not want you to worry about me. Nothing will happen to me. Look what I brought you: a nice plate of spaghetti and sauce, meatballs, salad, cheese, and bread."

Salvatore asked his wife, "When did you have time to cook?"

"Before coming here today," she replied, "I wasn't sleepy and was so excited to come here and see you, so I wanted to bring you a good meal. So, enjoy it!"

Salvatore thanked his wife. He then kissed and hugged his wife, bringing her towards the mattress.

Salvatore did not stop kissing and embracing her, removed her clothes, and they made passionate love, remaining in each other's arms.

Salvatore did not want to separate from his wife. The fragrant odor of her soft white skin made him feel as if he were dreaming.

Suddenly, he said, "Fortunata, are you here with me, or am I dreaming?"

Fortunata replied, "No, amore, you are not dreaming. I am really by your side and incredibly happy to spend time with you."

She continued, "I am sorry that I must leave you again. I must go before dawn. I promise that I will come back to visit you soon."

Salvatore did not want his wife to leave. He was so incredibly happy to see her and to have spent several magical hours with her.

Salvatore kissed Fortunata and said, "Thank you, amore, I feel so much better now. I understand that you must leave."

He went on, "I will be anxiously awaiting your next visit. Please kiss the children for me. Say hello to my father and remain alert."

At 8:00 in the morning the following day, he heard the whistle of a man who was singing and walking over to where Bastiano's men were hidden.

Bastiano, who was visiting his brother at that moment, realized that nothing could be happening at that time.

Therefore, to defend Salvatore, he signaled to his men that they should wait in the underbrush. Right away, his men ran into the road, visibly holding their weapons.

Seeing this man, who was still walking towards them, fired a shot.

They said, "Stop, or we will shoot you."

Salvatore heard the shot while, at the same time, he felt his body racked with pain as if he had been shot.

In the meantime, Bastiano ran over to the man approaching them.

He asked the man, "Who are you? Who has sent you? Are you aware that you could die soon? Answer me and inform me if any other men are here besides you!"

Shaking and frightened, the man replied, "My name is Giovanni. There is nobody here with me or following me. I am just lost and do not know where I am. I have a new job and am supposed to be there at 8:00."

Giovanni, still shaking, continued, "I cannot find the place where the job is located, and I do not know what to do. Help me, please. Help me find the right direction. I am so sorry if I have caused any suspicion. Please do not harm me! I am a married man and father of three children, and I want to work to earn some extra money."

Bastiano replied, placing his hands upon the man's shoulders, "Well, this is your lucky day. If you do what I ask, you will live."

He continued, "This is the way to go. Follow this sign, and you will find yourself again where you were in the beginning before you came here."

"Now, I must warn you," Bastiano goes on, "And this is especially important. If anyone asks you anything, you do not know anything. You have not seen or heard of anyone or anything. You will live a long time. Good luck."

Giovanni replied, "Yes, yes. I promise. I have seen nothing. I have not heard anything. Thank you," and he left.

That morning was chilly, but for Bastiano, it was okay. He returned to his brother with a preoccupied air. He said, "Everything went well."

Salvatore said, "I heard shooting and thought it was directed at me.

Salvatore felt better after Bastiano explained what had happened.

Bastiano tells his brother, "I will think of what we must do for you to be free and return with your family. Now, I must leave. I will return in a few days." They say goodbye and part ways.

CHAPTER 13

A month later, Salvatore finally reunites with his wife. He spends every moment possible making love and talking with her.

Together, they pray that this bad dream will pass soon and that everything will return to normal. Winter is approaching quickly. Each day that goes by, the mountains fill with a new storm, and rain covers the streets.

Salvatore begins to feel dread, knowing his wife must leave him. They share a passionate kiss.

"Be careful, my love," Salvatore says gently to his wife.

"Don't worry," she responds, "Ciao, I will see you soon."

Salvatore, inside the cave, returns to lie down on his mattress and intensely looks around. Thinking of his wife and children, he falls asleep and starts to have dreams of his mother, who died when he was eight years old.

His mother holds him close and says, "Do not be sad, my son; everything will be resolved."

She continues, "In one month, you will be free. I will stay close to you and will always protect you."

After not seeing her for so long, Salvatore woke up feeling happy to have dreamt about his mother. Even though it was only a dream, she gave him courage, patience, peace, and hope.

Three days pass, and Bastiano arrives to visit Salvatore. He has brought a friend with him and some men. He is carrying a rifle and two pistols in his belt.

"I have an idea for tomorrow," Bastiano said to Salvatore and his bodyguard. "You must follow my orders tonight so that you can be free tomorrow."

Salvatore does not understand what is happening, but he listens to his brothers' orders. All the men prepare to travel down the mountain to head into San Nicola L'arena.

The men are heavily armed. Salvatore is between two bodyguards and surrounded by ten other men who have all served as great mafia leaders. They reach about 50 meters outside the village to meet Bastiano and his men.

From there, Salvatore sees a large, dark car parked near the road with three men standing outside. He asks, "Why is that car there?"

One of the three men answers, "We have a surprise for you and your bodyguards. Please come inside to see."

One of the men opens the door. Salvatore immediately recognizes the man inside. It is the carabinieri who had fallen into the ravine. Another man is sitting next to him.

Frightened, Salvatore asks, "What does this mean?! Have you deceived me?!" as he tries to run from the men.

"Calm down, Salvatore," says one of the men, "No one has deceived you. This is good for you. He is handcuffed. We took him so he cannot testify against you in court."

The man continues to explain, "The man sitting next to him is your lawyer. We have made the carabinieri a proposal that he cannot refuse."

"Bastiano promised him that we will not kill him, but only if he leaves and never looks for you again. We will also give him money to start a new life far away from here."

"Are you sure about all of this?" asks Salvatore.

"We are very sure," answers the lawyer, "I guarantee that you will not see him in court or anywhere else. He knows what will happen to him if you do. Now, get in the car and enjoy the view."

Salvatore and the rest of the men go for a drive towards Trabia.

Trabia is the city after San Nicola L'arena, where the carabinieri, marshal's office, and barracks are located.

An hour before they went for the drive, Bastiano and his men sealed all the roads leading to the city's center. It was very early in the morning, and the people of Trabia slept quietly.

Bastiano's men were careful and on high alert when approaching the office and barracks. Five of his men poured gasoline all around the buildings, while others broke the windows to pour more gasoline inside.

Once they were sure they had covered the buildings in enough gasoline, they prepared their escape before lighting the matches.

The men all threw their lit matches and fled. The fire immediately burst so large it engulfed the barracks and looked like hellfire.

The people living close to the buildings began waking up to the great light and powerful flames and ran outside.

"Fire! Fire! Help!" They all screamed in great fear of their homes being burned.

The firefighters finally arrived. They extinguished the flames, but it was too late. The office and barracks were completely destroyed, and nothing was left to save.

The fireman asked the people near them if they had seen or heard anything that could have caused the fire.

Everyone in the town was asleep, so nobody saw or heard what had happened before the flames began. No one ever figured out how the fire was started.

In the meantime, the car Salvatore was in drove past. "Incredible!" everyone in the car exclaimed in shock of the fire.

"Everything went exactly how we planned it," said Bastiano.

After about an hour passed, the men all met at the lawyer's office in Termini Imeresi to discuss the rest of their plans.

"Salvatore and his two bodyguards will remain with me in my home," the lawyer says to Bastiano, "I will do everything I can to be in court this week."

"Bastiano," the lawyer continues, "take the carabinieri with you and watch him ensure he doesn't try to escape. We will decide what to do with him after court."

"And my father?" asks Bastiano.

"Do not worry," the lawyer responds, "I will talk to him, and he too will be free. Now go. I will let you know everything after we go to court."

Chapter 14

It was early in the morning, and still, the light stretched out, dazzling the sheets, which seemed to fall like a wall of gold from the sun.

Salvatore looks out the office window, grateful that this bad dream will soon be over. He will no longer have to hide in the mountains and will be with his family.

Thinking this miracle is due to his brother, Bastiano says, "I will never forget what my brother has done for me and my family."

A week later, Don Nino, Salvatore, and the lawyer went to court. When the judge began asking Don Nino and his son if they were guilty of the crimes, they both answered, "Not guilty."

The district attorney gets up and tells the judge, "They are both guilty. They must pay for what they have done and for the death of the carabinieri."

The judge asks the district attorney, "What evidence do you have?"

The district attorney answers, "All the physical evidence was burned in a fire. These documents are no longer available. However, we have a witness who should be here to testify."

The judge asks, "Where is your witness?"

With a heavy sigh, the district attorney answered, "Our witness still has not arrived."

The judge responds, "At this time, there is just not enough evidence to charge the defendants with this crime."

The judge then turns to both father and son and states, "This case is now closed. You are both free to go." Don Nino and Salvatore felt immense joy that their nightmare was finally over.

They both thanked the lawyer. Salvatore embraces his father, saying, "I cannot believe this. Is this really all over, Papa?"

"Yes, my son, you are free, and we can go home and celebrate your return."

They said goodbye to the lawyer. Don Nino told him he would go to his house to close the account and that he had an extra gift for him. They shook hands, and everyone left.

Salvatore arrived in San Nicola with boundless joy. As soon as he saw his family, he embraced his wife and kids with tears in his eyes.

His wife asked why he was crying, and he answered, "These are tears of joy because I am incredibly happy to be home with you. I did not think I would ever be free. I owe my freedom to my brother, Bastiano."

Salvatore continued to his wife, "Fortunata, you understand that I must talk to my brother and thank him. My father does not know anything about this situation. I was thinking I would like to tell him everything. He would have to speak to my brother again if he knew what he did for us."

Fortunata responded, "Go and talk to your brother, and when you come back, I will prepare a hot bath for you. Also, a nice dinner for the whole family to celebrate your return and your freedom."

Salvatore goes to visit his brother and says, "Bastiano, my dear brother, there are not enough words to thank you for everything that you did for me and our father. Papa still does not know, and I do not know how he will react when I tell him."

Salvatore continued, "Whatever Papa decides, I will let you know. I will never forget what you did for me for the rest of my life. I will always be grateful for you."

"From now on, I always want to see you and talk to you, as do the brothers who love each other, and I do love you very much. Even my wife thanks you."

Bastiano replies, "Salvatore, I am proud of what I did because even if Papa drove me out of the house, I must say that we learned to be united in the family and to help each other among us. I do not hold a grudge against our father, even if he will never talk to me again.

He continued, "I forgive him and have done what was necessary for you and our father because you are my family, and I love you. Now, whatever he wants to do or decides is up to him."

"Salvatore, I love you and I wish you a world of happiness with your family. Do not worry about me I am fine. In fact, I want to tell you something: I really like this girl, and if she says yes, I will marry her. Her name is Marianna," says Bastiano.

Salvatore hugs Bastiano and tells him, "I am so happy for you, my brother, and wish you to make a nice family. Let me know the answer she gives you. If you get married, I promise I will attend your wedding. Now, I want to ask, what did you do with the carabinieri that you held prisoner and had to testify against?"

Bastiano replies, "The lawyer made him sign that he will go to prison if he returns here to cause problems. He did not present himself to testify and, therefore, has the possibility of being killed. He should not risk coming. We have given him enough money to make a new life far away from here."

Bastiano continued, "We put him on an airplane to South America, so do not think about it anymore. Go, enjoy your freedom and your family."

They say goodbye, and Salvatore returns home, where his wife awaits him.

After Salvatore has relaxed and had a nice bath, he meets with his family to celebrate his return with a nice lunch and wine.

The children were happy to have their father with them. Mariella and little Ariana had fun playing with him, and Salvatore was happy to play with them.

The next day, Salvatore tells his father, "Papa, I must talk to you. It is important, and you must listen to me."

Don Nino looks at him and says, "What do you need to talk about? Is something wrong?"

Salvatore responds, "I must talk to you about my brother Bastiano, and please do not stop me from talking. You must know what Bastiano did for me and you."

Don Nino looks at his son and says, "What does Bastiano have to do with anything?"

Salvatore responds, "Bastiano saved you and me. It was he who helped me and brought me everything I needed in the mountains. It was he who made me come to church and see my family."

He continued, "It was Bastiano who left his men to protect me, and it was he who set fire to the barracks and ensured all of the documents were destroyed. He was the one who removed the carabinieri so he would not be there to testify, and it is because of him that you and I are free. Tell me, Papa, what do you have to say about your son Bastiano?"

Don Nino looks at Salvatore and says, "I will do my duty and I will give him a great gift, but regarding talking to him, this does not change anything. My father taught us and made us promise not to be involved with the Mafia, and he disobeyed me. This, I will never forgive him."

Salvatore responds to his father, "I am disappointed, Papa, with your decision. I cannot tell you what to do or make you change your mind, but I must tell you that I will continue to talk to my brother, and you cannot stop me. I will never forget what my brother did for me."

"Very well," Don Nino answers, "Tomorrow, I will tell you what I must do, and you will report back to your brother. Now, we go home."

CHAPTER 15

The next day, Don Nino went to meet with his lawyer, Mormino.

As Don Nino finished paying the lawyer for his services, he said, "I would like to give you an extra gift for all you have done for my son and me."

The lawyer, Mormino, replies, "Thank you. I am pleased to have helped you and grateful for this gift. If you should ever need me in the future, my door is always open to you."

Don Nino answers, "Yes. I need another favor. Today, I brought a contract from a property with nine acres of olive trees. I would like to give it to my son Bastiano as a gift for all he has done for my son and me.

He continues, "This would need to be done today so tomorrow Salvatore can bring it with a letter of appreciation thanking him for everything. I will appreciate your help and pay you for this favor I ask of you."

Mormino answers, "This is no problem. I will do it immediately. The notary can be here in half an hour to have this signed."

"Thank you," Don Nino replies.

The lawyer began preparing the papers. When he was done, the notary arrived to complete the signatures and stamp the seal.

Mormino then returns the contract to Don Nino and pays him again for help. Don Nino says thank you again and returns home to San Nicola.

Father and Sons

There, Don Nino seeks out his son Salvatore.

When he finds him, Don Nino says, "Take this envelope to your brother and thank him for me. Let him know that this is a gift for what he has done for us. Also, give him this message. Tell him I still never want to see or talk to him again."

Salvatore does not understand his father. But he knows that he must obey. So, he takes the envelope and goes to his brother Bastiano.

When he arrived, Bastiano was surprised to see him so soon. He asks Salvatore, "What has happened why are you here."

Salvatore replies, "I have brought you an envelope and a message from our father."

Bastiano answers, "What is the message, and why do you have this envelope."

Salvatore says, "Go ahead and open it, and I will tell you the message."

Bastiano opens the envelope and finds a contract stating that a 9-acre property of olive trees now belongs to him, with his father's appreciation for what he did.

Bastiano could not believe his eyes. As he turned to Salvatore, he said, "Everything I did was out of the kindness of my heart. I never asked or expected anything in return."

Salvatore responds, "Accept this gift then for your wedding. Now I would like to ask you a question. Has the girl responded to your question with the answer you were looking for."

"Yes," Bastiano said, "We will be getting married in one month."

"Congratulations! I am happy for you. I promise I will be at your wedding," Salvatore replies.

Bastiano answers, "Of course, you will be there because I am making you my best man."

Salvatore says, "It would be my pleasure. As for our father, do not expect him to be there. Furthermore, the message I mentioned earlier comes from our father."

Salvatore continues, "He told me that I should remind you that unless you leave the Mafia and live a normal life, he does not want to see or talk to you until then."

"I have a message for my father as well. Tell him I am happy with my life and will continue to be a part of the Mafia. While you are at it, tell him to check with his brother Turiddu," Bastiano replies.

"For, even he is in the Mafia. But his brother Turiddu is doing terrible things with his power. The people are cursing him. They are tired of receiving mystery letters, which are of Turridu asking for money, threatening that he will kill their animals or hurt the families if they do not pay. If father wants to know more, I will give you more information to give to him. At least I am using my power for good and giving back to the people."

Salvatore responds, "I am shocked and disappointed to hear about this. Are you sure he participates in these actions?"

"Yes," Bastiano responds.

Salvatore shook his head and said, "Let me process this information, and I will follow up with you soon."

After hearing this news, Salvatore went to find and speak with his father. He hoped his father would act and stop his uncle from further involvement with the Mafia.

Salvatore arrives home and finds his father is not there. He asks his mother-in-law where he can find his father.

Maria says, "He's at the farm."

Father and Sons

Salvatore thanks Maria and rushes out the door toward their farm.

Salvatore runs to his father and tells him he has important news to share.

"Papa, I heard something that will upset you, but you need to know the truth."

Don Nino looked up at his son, listening intensely to what his son was about to say.

Breathing heavily, Salvatore asks his father, "When was the last time you spoke with your brother Turiddu? How was he behaving? Did he act normal?"

Don Nino responds, "Why are you asking these questions? I see him three times a week, and I have not noticed anything different in his behavior."

Salvatore continues, "I have recently learned that he is sending individual anonymous letters to families. These letters demand that they deliver cash at a specific time and location. Then it says if they do not pay, he is threatening the families harm by burning their property, killing their livestock, and hurting their families."

Don Nino steps closer to his son, fists clenched, and jaw tightened. He asks, "WHO DID YOU HEAR THIS FROM?"

"Bastiano told me today. He will share more information with you through me if you want more information. He asks me if you will be confronting Turiddu about these allegations."

Don Nino shook his head angrily and said, "Yes, I will confront him. When I get home tonight, I will find him, discuss this matter, and see what he has to say about it."

He puts his hand on Salvatore's shoulder and continues, "My son, I cannot believe my brother has dishonored our father's last request. We all committed and promised we would not follow the life of the Mafia. We would live honestly, taking care of our families, friends, and our community. Thank you for sharing this news, I will let you know how he reacts and responds to our conversation."

Don Nino arrives home and tells his wife to plan a late dinner. He has some business he wants to discuss with his brother. He showers and then heads over to his brother's home. As he knocks on the door, Turiddu opens it.

Turridu smiles happily, "What a surprise! How are you? What brings you here?"

Don Nino intensely looks into his eyes and responds, "I am here to speak with you, and I expect the truth."

He continued, "Do you remember our promise to our father before he passed?"

"What promise are you referring to exactly?" Turiddu asks.

"The promise to live a tranquil, honest, and respectful life. The promise to make the right decision and not follow a mafia lifestyle. So…

Do you have something to tell me?" Don Nino asks his brother as he looks him in the eyes.

Turiddu raises his voice and answers, "I don't have anything to say, and I don't understand what you are accusing me of doing."

A silent, long pause.

He says, "Yes, I remember our promise to our father. We have all respected and followed his wishes. Can I offer you a glass of wine and some cheese?"

Don Nino responds, "I am interested in what you have to offer. I came to see if you would be transparent and truthful, but instead, you deny it all."

He continues, "Turiddu, our father left us with enough property and money to live a profitable and comfortable life.

I advise you to work honestly and ethically. The truth will always arise, and our secrets will eventually surface. If you do not change, I fear you may experience things you do not expect, and then it will be too late."

Don Nino goes on, "Anna Maria, Maria Angela, Giovanni, Ignazio, and I have kept our promise to live the life our father hoped. You are the only one of us that has gone down the brutal path. I am here to support and help you change your ways. I hope you are listening to my words and making the right choice. If you choose to continue down this path, I consider you DEAD to me. Do not expect any help from your family. We will no longer have anything to do with you."

Time stood still.

Don Nino did not wait for a response from his brother. He turned and walked away.

That evening, he shared dinner with his family.

After dinner, Don Nino asked his son to follow up with Bastiano and gather as much information about Turiddu's mafia dealings.

He asked his son to report back to him. Then hugged him and wished him goodnight.

Salvatore responds, "I will see him tomorrow and report back any information I gather from our conversation."

The following day, Salvatore went to visit his brother. Bastiano was excited to see him and welcomed him in.

"I spoke to Papa, and he had visited his brother Turiddu yesterday. Turiddu denied having any connection with the Mafia. Papa did not believe him and gave him the same threat he said to you. If you recall, he said that if you do not choose to live a normal and honest life, he will no longer have anything to do with you for the rest of his life. These words were repeated to Turiddu." Salvatore said.

He continued, "It was Papa that sent me to speak to you. He asked me to find out everything you know about Turiddu regarding his connections and dishonest business."

"This is what I can tell you," Bastiano responded. "Uncle Turiddu has been manipulating his daughter to write letters anonymously, sending them to people in our community. He is asking them for cash payments and threatening their lives if they do not pay. I am aware of where he is asking people to drop off the money in an unmarked white envelope."

Bastiano continues, "Do you remember the small chapel next to our church? This is where people go and pray to the Virgin Mary. The people are asked to leave the envelope behind this statue, and he will pick all the envelopes up at night."

Bastiano continues telling his brother that he has proof of many people in the community begging him for help.

Several people in the community have requested that Bastiano ask his father to get involved and stop Turiddu from making these demands.

Turiddu has caused so much sadness and stress. People have lost livestock, and he has burned down farms. The community is praying that this will end.

They have even said they are hoping that the person writing these letters can no longer use their hands and, as a result, stop writing these threats.

Bastiano concludes, "Everyone is praying for a miracle, wanting to see Turiddu move on with a horrible death. They all want to live a tranquil and peaceful life."

Salvatore is in shock as he listens to his brother speak. He told him that he would share all this information with their father.

Then Salvatore asks, "Is there anything you can do to help our people and stop our uncle?"

"Personally, there is nothing I can physically do to stop him, but I do have an acquaintance I reached out to, and he has a plan to stop Turiddu. He will get back to me in a few weeks to give us a chance to try to have Turiddu reconsider his actions." Bastiano says to him.

Bastiano hugged his brother and told Salvatore to return home and discuss all he had learned with their Papa.

Chapter 16

Salvatore was still in shock and could not believe what he had learned about his uncle.

He was waiting impatiently to see his father so that he could share these new facts that he learned. He knew he would be at the farm at this time of day, so he began to take the walk.

As he reached his father, tears were running down his face from what he learned from his conversation with his brother.

Don Nino looks at his son and immediately knows the information his son has received is draining him emotionally. He asks him to have a seat, take a deep breath, and slowly explain to him what he has discovered.

Salvatore began to give details of what he had learned. He talked about how his uncle was manipulating his own daughter, Puretta.

As a schoolteacher, she is educated and has the writing skills to write the letters that have threatened the people.

Salvatore also told his father about the damage Turiddu was causing livestock and farms and the harm he was causing those who did not pay.

As Salvatore continued, he revealed how the people had been coming to Bastiano and begging him to end the fear and terror that Turiddu was causing in the town.

He then shared that the people are asking not only for Bastiano to support them but for Don Nino to help as well.

Father and Sons

As Don Nino listened to his son, he could not believe what he was hearing. He was angry that he had asked his brother about these allegations, and his brother denied having anything to do with these letters or the damage they had caused to their community.

Don Nino told his son he was grateful for all the information he and Bastiano had shared, and he said, "I know now what I must do!"

Salvatore looked like his father and said, "Papa, please be careful and think through what you are planning. I do not want any harm to come to you."

Don Nino lives an honest life. He has always helped anyone in need. He is a good man with friends across his country who will always support him with any request.

He reached out to well-regarded friends in Palermo. His thought was to share the information he gathered and get their advice on how to manage this matter. Don Nino left to meet with his friends.

They collaborated on a plan to stop Turiddu and the continued threat and chaos he was causing their people.

Don Nino returns home. He sits down and contemplates what may happen. He has a moment to reflect and understands there is no turning back.

He knows that he can no longer speak or think about the facts that led his brother to this outcome. He and his family will continue to live their lives as if none of their findings existed.

As Salvatore and his father are working on the farm, Salvatore turns to his father and says, "Papa, I have some wonderful news to share. My wife and I are expecting our third child."

With a strong embrace, Don Nino grabbed his son and said, "My son, this is the best news you could have shared!" At that moment, Don Nino is in a place where he does not think about his brother.

He continues, "Let us finish early and head home. We have a celebration to plan for a new grandchild who will be arriving."

As they arrive home, Don Nino embraces his daughter-in-law, Fortunata, and continues to show his excitement about his newest grandchild. That night, the whole family has a feast and shares a toast celebrating the pregnancy.

A few weeks have passed since the family shared the news of the new baby. An invitation arrives for another happy event celebrating Bastiano's wedding.

Bastiano asked his brother to be his best man. Salvatore asked his wife if she was feeling well enough to attend the wedding.

Fortunata responds, "Did you tell your Papa about the wedding?"

"Yes," Salvatore responds, "My Papa will not stop me from attending the wedding as the best man because he knows how much Bastiano has done for me and our family."

In agreement, they decided to attend the wedding. As the next three weeks passed, every day was enjoyed, and the family continued to live their lives.

One evening, Don Nino and his son were heading home after a long workday on their farm. As Don Nino walked into his home, his wife ran toward him, trembling as she shared she had heard some tragic news.

Don Nino immediately assumed the news was about his daughter-in-law and her baby. He shouted back, "Did something happen to Fortunata?"

Maria assures him that Fortunata and the baby are healthy and safe.

"The Tragedy has to do with your brother," she continues. Rosina came over crying today and told me that her husband had received a package in the mail marked "URGENT! OPEN IMMEDIATELY!"

"Your brother opened the package and was attacked and bitten by a venomous snake. When Rosina arrived home, she found her husband on the floor and immediately called the doctor."

Maria continues, "When the doctor arrived, he told Rosina that her husband was already dead, and the cause of death looked to be from several poisonous bites he found on his body. I called Rosina's children, and they came over quickly. They found a box with a note inside that read:

This is for you for all the harm you have caused these poor people!!!!!

Maria asks Don Nino, "What does this note mean? What harm are they talking about?"

Don Nino responds, "Maria, I will tell you later. Right now, we must help Rosina."

They removed the body of Turiddu and sprayed the inside and outside of the house with poison to make sure that the snake would die.

Since it was necessary for no people or animals to be in the house while the poison was there, Don Nino let his sister-in-law Rosina stay in his house during this time.

The following day, they returned to the house and found the snake dead. After cleaning and disinfecting, Rosina was able to return home.

Three days later, they had Turiddu's funeral. Don Nino told Rosina, "If you need anything, please let me know, and I will help you."

"Thank you," Rosina responded, "for all the help you and your wife have given me."

All the people who used to receive anonymous letters felt more relaxed when they found out that Turiddu died, but they were also sad because they didn't want him to die.

Each of them said a prayer when he died. They prayed for Turiddu and thanked God they wouldn't receive these letters asking for money anymore. They were happy that they could continue to live a more tranquil life.

A few days after Turiddu's funeral, Rosina saw her brother-in-law, Don Nino.

She asked him to explain the best he could about her husband's debt, from the note and everything else that's been going on that she is not aware of.

Rosina said, "Nino, please, I think you know more than you are saying about what happened with your brother. Can you please explain to me everything you know, including the death of my husband, the snake, the note, and the package?"

She continues, "The only thing I know is that when you came to my house and asked Turiddu a lot of questions, you were not happy with the answers he gave you, and you left very upset. Can you please explain everything that has happened to me?"

Don Nino responded, "Rosina, please sit down, and I'll explain everything to you. Your husband was sending anonymous letters to different families. He was asking for money in these letters. If they didn't pay, he threatened to kill their animals, damage their farm, or even hurt the families."

He continues, "Those people are very tired and very angry. They have prayed daily for him to stop sending those letters because they couldn't handle it anymore."

"Everyone works very hard to help their families, put a roof over their heads, and put food on the table for their kids. The money they made was enough for their families, but when they had to pay him, they had nothing left for themselves."

Don Nino continued, "Rosina, what would you have done if you had been in their place? How would you have felt? I tried to convince him to stop this kind of life when I found out. I even reminded him that he was dishonoring the promise that we made to our father on his deathbed. We promised that we would not be involved in the Mafia. He did not listen to me and denied to me his involvement. Now you know everything, Rosina. I feel bad for you, but this is the truth."

Rosina responded, "Thank you for explaining everything to me. I cannot believe that my husband was living this kind of life."

They said goodbye, and Rosina left to return to her house. As she was walking home, she wondered how her husband could have been doing all of this, and nobody knew.

Rosina didn't know, and Nino didn't tell her that her daughter Puretta also knew what was happening.

Puretta was writing the letters, but her father threatened her to keep her mouth shut. Puretta felt bad and did not want to do this, but her father forced her to.

Now, even Puretta is suffering because of all the curses that the people are sending her. Puretta got a sickness in her hands, so her hands would shake so badly that she could not hold anything without dropping it.

CHAPTER 17

As some time passed, the day quickly arrived for Bastiano to get married. Mariella, the oldest daughter of Salvatore and Fortunata, is the flower girl, and Salvatore is his best man.

It was a good wedding. Everything went well, and they had a great party. Everyone was at the party except Don Nino because he still refused to speak with his son.

Bastiano and his bride Marianna went to Italy for their honeymoon, and after one year, Bastiano and his wife had a little girl that they named Maria.

In the meantime, Fortunata had her third child, another little girl. They called her Vittoria. She was a beautiful little girl with big black eyes, curly hair, and beautiful, delicate skin.

Everyone was happy, especially Don Nino, who threw a big, beautiful party for her baptism.

The two sisters, Mariela and Ariana, were very happy to have another little sister. They always wanted to stay close to her, especially Ariana, who wanted to protect her.

Ariana grew up very delicate; she was not able to eat very much, and when her mother forced her to eat, it would cause her to vomit.

Fortunata was bothered because Ariana was not eating, so she made an appointment with the family doctor in Palermo.

The months went by, and Vittoria was growing in good health. When Vittoria was seven months old, Fortunata had an appointment in Palermo to take Ariana to the doctor.

Fortunata asked her sister-in-law Francesca if she could look after Vittoria while she took Ariana to the appointment in Palermo.

Francesca responded, "Yes, of course, I can look after Vittoria; it is my pleasure. Today is a beautiful day, and as I do some embroidering, she can sit close to me, and her beautiful cheeks will get rosy. Do what you must do, and do not worry about Vittoria. We'll see each other when you come back."

"Thank you," Fortunata said to Francesca, "Please be careful."

Fortunata and Ariana went to catch the train to Palermo. When they arrived, Fortunata asked the doctor, "Doctor, what can I do to get Ariana to eat? Do you see how skinny she is? She faints all the time. Please help me; I don't want to lose my daughter."

The doctor responded, "Fortunata, tell me. Is there anything that your daughter likes to eat?"

Fortunata responded, "The only thing she seems to want to or be able to eat is fruit. She does not vomit when she eats fruit."

The doctor said, "Fortunata, don't push her to eat other things. If she only wants to eat fruit, then she is getting what her body needs from the fruit. In time, she will start to eat other foods."

Fortunata thanked the doctor, and they left to get the train back to San Nicola.

In the meantime, back in the small town, Francesca and Vittoria were sitting in front of the house near the street, where all the cars pass by.

During this time in 1944, when there was a need to transport groups of animals from one place to another, there was no other way besides this street through the small town.

Suddenly, there was one group of sheep with a dog and their owner, followed by a group of cows with a dog and their owner passing through the street where Francesca and Vittoria were sitting.

Francesca had no time to take the baby inside, so she remained where she was.

Suddenly, she hears Vittoria scream. She turns to see a little blood on Vittoria's cheek. Francesca didn't understand how this could have happened.

After she cleaned her cheek, she noticed a little red spot remained. Francesca and Vittoria continued sitting outside even after all the animals had passed.

In the meantime, Fortunata and Ariana arrived back home. Fortunata said thank you to Francesca, took Vittoria, and went back inside the house.

Fortunata noticed Vittoria had a red mark on her cheek and returned to talk to Francesca.

"Francesca, what happened to Vittoria's cheek? Maybe you poked the baby with the needle?"

"No," responded Francesca, and she explained everything that happened with all the animals passing by the street.

Fortunata could not believe what Francesca was saying and was not thinking about what could possibly happen later.

Later that evening, Fortunata noticed that Vittoria was not eating. She looked worn down like she just wanted to go to sleep.

Fortunata was worried, so she took Vittoria to the doctor in Palermo the next day.

When the doctor saw Vittoria's worn-out appearance, he started to perform some tests. He noticed that something had poked Vittoria's cheek.

He asked, "Fortunata, what has happened with your daughter?"

Fortunata explained what Francesca had told her: maybe an insect from the animals had bitten her cheek.

"I'm sorry, Fortunata," the doctor said, "but the baby has poison in her blood from the insect that bit her. We cannot save her."

Fortunata looked at the doctor and said, "Yesterday, the baby was ok. Only 24 hours have passed by. I do not understand, doctor. Please help me. See if you can save my baby."

The doctor started to talk to Fortunata; he put his hand on her shoulder.

"The baby cannot be saved," he said, "return home, and for the time you have left with Vittoria, stay close to her, and try to resign. I'm sorry."

Fortunata cried. She held Vittoria tight to her chest, returned home, and told everyone the news about what the doctor said.

She went into a room with the baby and closed the door. She kept Vittoria close to her chest, cried, kissed the baby, and prayed to Jesus for a miracle.

She said, "Jesus, please, I pray for a miracle. I don't want to lose my daughter." As she prayed, she thought about how Vittoria was in such good health, and in just two days, everything changed.

Fortunata didn't want to go to sleep. She sat in the rocking chair, closed her eyes, and said, "Jesus, please, I ask you for a miracle to save my baby," and then she fell asleep.

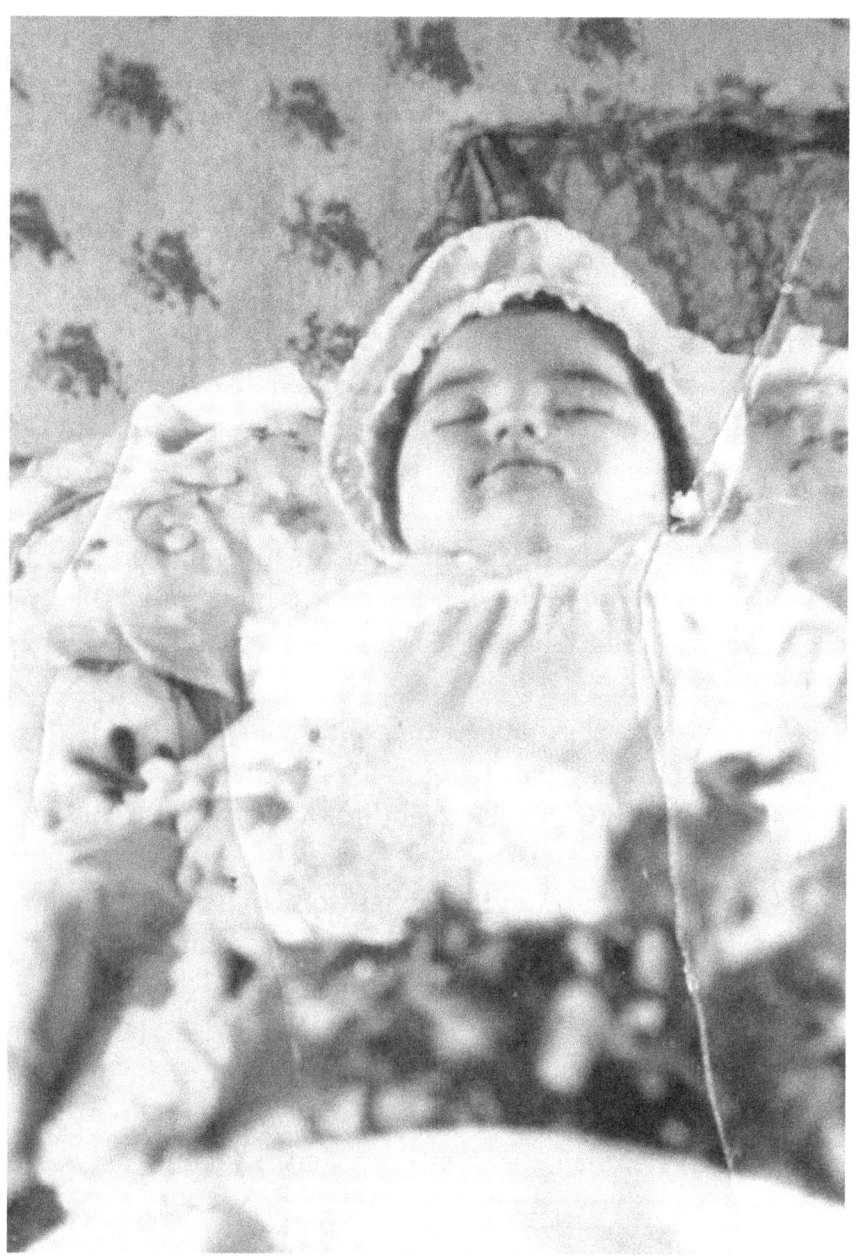

Vittoria

As she slept, she dreamed that she was playing with Vittoria, but suddenly, Vittoria was gone. She did not see or hear her anymore. She yelled, "Vittoria, Vittoria, where are you?"

As she woke up from her dream, she realized that the baby was no longer alive, and that is why she could not see her in her dream anymore.

Her youngest daughter died in her arms.

One cannot imagine the incredible pain that Fortunata was feeling in her heart to have lost such a beautiful baby as Vittoria, who was in such very good health and, two days later, dead.

At only seven months, she became an angel of God.

Ariana could not understand what was happening; she was only two years old. She was confused as she did not see her sister or hear her cry.

The next day, she noticed that Vittoria, dressed in white, including a little hat, was lying in the middle of the table.

A beautiful white tablecloth embroidered by Fortunata was on the table under the baby.

In Sicily, it is tradition that when somebody dies, they are placed in the middle of the first room you enter, and people come to visit and offer their condolences to the family.

Everybody that came to visit the beautiful, dead baby felt a lot of sorrow. They tried to give courage to Fortunata, brought a lot of flowers, and kissed her on the head.

Between them all, they said, "What a shame to lose a beautiful baby in two days, especially because before, she was in good health."

Ariana stayed close to her mother. She was crying and kept pulling her mother's dress because she did not understand why her sister was in the middle of the table and why all this attention was on Vittoria. She felt that nobody was paying any attention to her.

Finally, Fortunata took her in her arms because she would not stop crying.

Ariana felt much better when she was in her mother's arms and could see her sister, Vittoria, and everyone who came to visit her.

Ariana did not understand what had happened to Vittoria; she thought Vittoria was asleep.

Suddenly, she said, "Mamma, why is Vittoria still sleeping? When will my little sister wake up?"

Fortunata and some guests started to cry; they were affected by what Ariana said.

Fortunata did not know how to respond to Ariana; she was too young to understand that Vittoria was dead.

The next day, they brought the little casket for Vittoria. The casket was all white.

Ariana's father took her to another room to try to calm her down. He tried to explain that her sister had become an angel of God and gone to heaven.

Ariana responded "Papa, I want to go too."

Her father said, "No, honey, it's not your time. You will see. When you are asleep, your sister will come and see you, and she will stay with you all night. But during the day, you cannot see her."

Ariana said, "Papa, I don't want to stay alone with Mamma. She always cries all the time. I want to stay with you."

Her father replied, "Ok, honey. From now on, you can come with me every time I go to the farm. Now, you must be a good girl and listen because we must go to the church to say goodbye to Vittoria."

Father and Sons

    Don Nino, all the family, and all the friends were walking behind the casket. Four young boys dressed in white carried the casket into the church.

    Many went to pay their respects at the funeral for the baby. After the funeral, they went to the cemetery to bury her.

CHAPTER 18

The house of Don Nino was not the same. Nobody laughed or joked around. Everyone was sad because they had lost Vittoria.

As time passed, life continued. Everybody went back to work and carried on.

Fortunata decided to teach some young girls how to design and embroider to help time continue moving and keep herself occupied so she would not be so sad.

Salvatore would take Ariana to the farm with him three times a week because she did not want to stay with her mamma.

One day, as Salvatore and Ariana came back home, the sky was very dark with many clouds. Salvatore understood that the weather was getting bad, so he tried to go fast with the Carretto Siciliano and mule.

Suddenly, it started to rain very hard, and he did not have time to find a place to go so they would not get wet.

When they arrived home, they were both soaking wet. Fortunata immediately grabbed Ariana, removed her clothes, and brought her to the tub for a warm bath. Salvatore did the same.

The next day, Ariana was very sick with a high fever. Fortunata was upset and told her husband, "You cannot take her with you anymore. If she dies, it will be your fault. I do not want to lose another daughter. I am still mourning the loss of my baby Vittoria!"

She continues, saying, "You better pray to Jesus that Ariana will be ok. And you will never take her with you to the farm again."

Salvatore responded, "Fortunata, stay calm. Ariana will be ok. I promise you I will not take her with me anymore."

A couple of days later, Ariana was better. One evening, she told her father, "Papa, I want to go with you tomorrow morning. I am not sick anymore. I feel much better now."

As Ariana spoke to her father, Fortunata overheard what she was saying. She turned to her daughter and said, "No, my darling. You cannot go; you must stay with me."

Fortunata continued, "Papa cannot take you with him anymore because he has a lot of work to do."

Ariana responded, "No, I don't want to stay with you because you are always sad and cry all the time. I like staying with Papa better."

Fortunata paused and said, "If I don't cry anymore, will you stay with me?"

"Yes, Mamma. But you must promise me."

Fortunata responded, "Yes, tesoro. I promise you." She hugged and kissed her, and together, they started to smile.

CHAPTER 19

In 1946, the small town of San Nicola had no doctor, pharmacy, or hospital. If somebody needed to see a doctor, they would have to take the train to Palermo.

Maria, the wife of Don Nino and mother of Fortunata, had a gift from God to help anybody who needed help. She had a lot of courage and an instinct to do whatever she had to do.

For example, if somebody needed stitches in their head, she would clean it and put a lot of pure white sugar where they needed stitches. Enough so the bleeding would stop. After a couple of days, they returned to her; she would clean it, disinfect it, and the wound would be healed.

Another example is when somebody has tooth pain or infection, she suggests boiling some lettuce. When the water was cold, to remove the water, put the lettuce in the mouth for 30 minutes, and it would remove their pain or infection.

Another suggestion is that if somebody has indigestion or stomach pain, they should get a lemon, squeeze it in a glass, add water until it is almost full, and then add one small spoon of sugar and one small spoon of baking soda.

Maria once helped a man with a splinter in his eye. She removed it without a problem, and he called her Angel Maria.

Another man caught a fish, but it was still alive. He tried to bite the fish to kill it, but instead, the fish went inside and got stuck in his throat. They took him right away to see Maria. She was able to remove the fish and save his life. After removing the fish, she said, "It was a miracle that God helped me."

Maria also had another gift for helping the poor. If she saw a child without shoes, she would go home and talk to the mother, giving enough money for new shoes and food for the whole family.

The people always thanked her, which earned her a lot of respect. Maria was happy to help anybody who needed it.

Some time passed, and life went on as normal, and everything went well.

In the summer, Fortunata cooked the tomatoes to make the sauce for the winter. Once they were cold, she put them in glass jars.

Every Sunday, she used one jar to make sauce with meatballs and cook spaghetti. This Sunday tradition was enjoyed by all.

One day, Ariana was playing with the pots, pans, and spoons, making a lot of noise. Suddenly, she heard a big "Boom!" like a gunshot.

Ariana was so scared she started to scream, fell to the floor, and held her breath in terror. Her mother heard the loud noise, not knowing what it was, and ran to Ariana to make sure she was alright.

Fortunata found Ariana on the floor and saw that she was black in color. Fortunata went to the balcony and tried to call for help.

"Help me! Somebody, please help me! I am going to lose my daughter!"

A woman was passing by and heard her screams. She went to see if she could help.

The woman saw Ariana on the floor, grabbed a bucket, and filled it with water. She then threw the water on top of Ariana.

Once Ariana felt the water, she started to shake, opened her eyes, and the color returned to her skin. She then began to cry.

Fortunata hugged Ariana and said, "Tesoro, what happened?" Ariana said, "Mamma, there was a big boom, and I was so scared."

Fortunata responded, "Do not be afraid anymore; I am here and will stay with you all the time. I will never leave you by yourself. You are safe now. We need to say thank you to this lady who helped save your life."

As Fortunata turned towards the woman, she said, "Thank you very much for saving my baby. I don't even know your name, what is it?"

The woman said, "My name is Nina."

Fortunata asked her, "How did you know you needed to throw water on the baby?"

Nina responded, "It was an instinct. The baby was so afraid she was holding her breath. That is why she started to get black. The water helped to revive her, and she started to breathe again. I am very happy I was able to help you."

From that day on, Fortunata and Nina became very good friends.

Chapter 20

As time passed, everything was going well—until one day when Bastiano did not feel good.

Bastiano asked his wife, Marianna, to call his stepmother, Maria, to see if she could help.

Marianna responded, "You do not need her! She is not even your mother. I am your wife, and I will help you!"

She did not call Maria and did not do anything to help her husband, and Bastiano started to get worse. He begged his wife to call Maria because he had a lot of faith in her and knew she would be able to help him. His wife refused to call Maria and did nothing to help him.

The woman who saved Ariana, Nina, lived next door to Bastiano.

She did not see Bastiano go in or out of his house for one month.

Nina went to see Fortunata and Salvatore and said, "Something is not right, Fortunata. I suggest you send your husband to see if Bastiano is ok."

Nina continued, "I knocked on the door, and nobody answered, so I decided to come here to tell you what is going on."

Maria heard what Nina said, and she said to them, "Instead of Salvatore, I will go myself to see what is going on. I will call you and let you know what happens."

Maria went to Bastiano's house. She knocked at the door, and Marianna opened the door. When Marianna saw Maria, she was very rude and said, "What do you want? What are you doing here? We don't need you!"

Maria pushed Marianna and went inside. She called, "Bastiano! Bastiano! Where are you? If you are here, answer me!"

Marianna was furious and grabbed Maria by the arm. Maria pushed Marianna back, and she fell to the floor.

The whole time, she kept calling "Bastiano! Bastiano! Answer me!"

Bastiano heard and recognized Maria's voice. He tried to say, "Mamma, I am here in the bedroom. Please help me."

Maria went to the bedroom and saw Bastiano. She got close to him and said, "My son. What has happened to you?"

Bastiano responded, "I had a little bump on my leg, and as the days passed, it grew and became more swollen. It became larger, more painful, and infected. I asked my wife to call you; she said she would help me instead. But she has done nothing for me."

As Maria turned to Marianna, she said, "You are very cruel and bad to your husband. If you did not want me to come, at least you could have taken him to the doctor in Palermo. You have never been a good wife. If something happens to Bastiano, it is all your fault. This will be on your conscience for the rest of your life!"

As Maria turned to Bastiano, she said, "I will do whatever I can, but I think that only Jesus can make this miracle. Bastiano, a lot of time has passed that something could have been done, but it's too late. You have a lot of infection in your body, and I don't think I can do anything. Just pray to God."

Bastiano looked at Maria and said, "Mamma, please help me. I trust you. You have been a very good second mother. You have taught me and my brother and sisters how to love and respect each other and treat everyone well. I have done my best in my life, and I hope that I did not disappoint you."

With tears in her eyes, Maria took Bastiano's hand, kissed his forehead, and said, "Thank you for calling me Mamma." Then she looked at his leg, cleaned it, and applied disinfecting antibiotics.

She said, "Who cut the skin around your wound?"

Bastiano responded, "My wife."

Maria said, "It was worse because she never disinfected the scissors. So, everything you are going through and your suffering are your wife's fault."

Maria said, "It's time for me to go. I will come back tomorrow."

Bastiano squeezed her hand and said, "Mamma, please don't go. I want you to stay close to me. Like when I was a little boy and was scared, you would stay close to me until I was asleep."

Maria looked at him and did not have the courage to tell him no.

She said to him, "Ok, my son. I will stay with you all night, holding your hand. I want you to be calm and happy."

He said, "Thank you, Mamma. I love you."

Maria called Mariella, Bastiano's daughter, and said, "Go call Ms. Nina, say to come here right away because I want to talk to her."

Mariella ran and called Ms. Nina. They came back together, and Maria explained everything that's happened.

She said, "Nina, please go to my daughter and tell them what has happened. I am staying here all night with Bastiano. This might be his last night."

"Of course, I'll do this," Nina replied.

Nina went to Fortunata's house and said, "Fortunata, I have some very bad news. Your mother is with Bastiano and will stay all night. She sent me here to explain what had happened. Bastiano is very sick and in very bad shape. He has a massive infection all over his body. His wife refused to let anybody know or help him. She did nothing to help and not take him to the doctor. Your mother is very upset that nobody called her because she would have taken him to the doctor herself."

Fortunata responded, "I feel bad for Bastiano. He does not deserve to suffer this way. Thank you for telling me. I will talk to my husband and father-in-law and tell them everything. I am so happy that my mother is staying with Bastiano. Thank you, Nina."

In the evening, when Don Nino and Salvatore returned home, Fortunata explained everything that Nina had told her.

She told them that Maria was staying all night with Bastiano.

Don Nino did not say anything, but Salvatore could not believe that his brother was going to die.

He said, "Fortunata, please let my father eat. I must go to my brother."

He turned to his father and said, "Papa, what are you doing? Do you want to come too?" Don Nino said, "No, send my regards."

When Salvatore arrived at Bastiano's house, he knocked on the door.

Mariella opened the door and said, "Hi, Uncle. Papa is not feeling good. He is in the bedroom. Nonna is with him."

"And your mother, where is she?" Salvatore asked Mariella.

"I don't know," said Mariella.

Salvatore went to the bedroom, and when he saw his brother, he hugged him.

He said, "I'm sorry. I feel so bad. But I am happy that Mamma is here with you. I will also stay here with you all night. I will pray that Jesus makes a miracle and that you will feel better tomorrow."

Bastiano, with a low and shaking voice, responded, "Thank you for coming. And thank you for staying here with Mamma and me. If I do not wake up tomorrow, I want you to know that I love you and that I will die happy."

Bastiano turned, looking at Maria, and said, "Mamma, I feel bad that I am leaving my daughter and everybody else. I was not lucky with my wife. If she loved me, she would have done anything to try and help me. She would have taken me to the doctor or called you when I asked you to help me."

Maria, on one side of the bed, and Salvatore, on the other side, as they held Bastiano's hand, they watched him die at 4 a.m.

Mariella was asleep, and Salvatore told Maria, "You stay here and take care of Mariella. I will go home and tell everyone. I will talk to my father to prepare for the funeral."

"Ok," Maria responded.

Marianna never came back. Maria went to the other bedroom and lay down with Mariella so she would not get scared if she awoke.

Salvatore and Don Nino made all the arrangements for the funeral, and after two days, they held the funeral for Bastiano.

He lost his life at 49 years of age, leaving behind one daughter.

Many people liked him because of everything he did to help when they needed it. The church was full of people; everyone from this small town was there to pay their respects to Bastiano.

Don Nino stayed home with the kids. Salvatore, his wife, his three sisters, their families, and Maria went to the funeral to honor Bastiano.

Marianna, Bastiano's wife, never came back home after she left.

She did not even think of her daughter. She never showed up for the funeral.

People started to talk; everybody was very disappointed that she was not at the funeral.

Many people said things like, "What kind of woman is she? She is cruel, with no respect for her husband or daughter."

CHAPTER 21

One year after Bastiano's death, Marianna married again. Together, they had another daughter, Rosetta.

When Don Nino finds out that she has remarried, he wonders if she has another lover while married to Bastiano.

Maybe that's why she would not help her husband when he was sick because she wanted him to die so she would become free to marry her lover.

Don Nino and his family decided they never wanted to see her, speak of her, or even mention her name again.

To them, she was dead, like Bastiano.

Time passed, life continued, work continued, and everything was normal.

After two years, Fortunata became pregnant with another baby. When she told her husband, Salvatore hugged her and said, "I am so happy; I can hardly wait to tell my father."

Fortunata said, "And I want to tell my mother."

When Don Nino and Salvatore went to work the next day, Salvatore said, "Papa, I have beautiful news that I want to share with you."

Don Nino responded, "Salvatore, my son. After all this tragedy and sadness, it's time to hear some good news. Tell me, what is going on?"

"Papa, my wife is expecting another baby!"

Don Nino hugged his son and said, "Thank you, my son, for this beautiful news! I am very happy. Please tell your wife to be careful."

Salvatore responded, "We are going to go home, and we are going to tell her tonight."

In the meantime, Fortunata went to talk to her mother to tell her the wonderful news.

She said, "Mamma, I must tell you something that I have not even told my husband. When I came back from the doctor with Vittoria, I was so sad that they could not save my baby because of her blood being poisoned. When I was home, I was so sad that I went to my room. It was just me and my baby in my arms, and as I cried, I fell asleep."

Fortunata continued her story, "As I slept, I dreamed I was playing with Vittoria, and she wanted to play hide-and-seek. Then, she said, 'Mamma, you will have another little girl after me.' I was never thinking about what she said to me. When I was looking for her and didn't see her anymore, I called her name over and over. When I woke up, Vittoria was dead in my arms."

Maria could not believe what Fortunata said but was so happy she was now pregnant with another baby.

She said, "My daughter, sometimes miracles happen. Jesus took one child from you, but he sent you another one. Vittoria became a beautiful angel from heaven to protect your family."

After three months, Fortunata got together with Mariella and Ariana, and she said, "My dears. I must tell you some beautiful news. You will have a baby sister or brother in a couple of months. How do you feel? Does this make you happy?"

"Yes, yes, Mamma! We are very happy!" the sisters said. Ariana responded, "Mamma, is Vittoria coming back to us?"

"No, Gioia," responded Fortunata, "Vittoria is a beautiful angel. But because she could not be here with us, she sent us another baby."

The sisters were very happy. Almost every day, they would ask their mother, "Mamma! When is the baby coming?"

"You have to have patience," Fortunata responded, "We need time because the baby is coming from very far away. Now you go play."

Finally, the day everyone was waiting for arrived. Fortunata gave birth, another little girl, and they called her Antonina Rosa.

Everything went well, and everybody was very happy, especially Ariana, who now had another little sister to look after.

She liked staying close to her and protecting her.

One day, Ariana asked her Mamma, "Mamma, is this little sister going to stay with us? Or will she become an angel like Vittoria?"

Fortunata responded, "No, Tesoro. Antonina Rosa will stay with us forever. When she grows up, you can play with her. Are you happy?"

"Yes, yes, Mamma! I am very, very happy!" Ariana exclaimed.

The days went by, and everything was normal. Everyone was happy.

Don Nino and Salvatore continued business on the farm. Fortunata was very busy with the children, but Mariella and Ariana started attending school. They were very happy children.

The following ten years passed, and the family seemed to have a very happy and normal life.

Until one day when Maria returned from church as she did every morning. When she came home, she told Ariana, "I don't feel good. Please call the doctor and send someone to call Nonno on the farm."

Antonina Rosa

Ariana put her grandmother in bed and immediately called the doctor. She also sent somebody to call her father and grandfather on the farm so she did not leave her grandmother alone.

In the meantime, the doctor arrived at the house. He saw Maria and said to Ariana, "Ariana, your grandmother is having a heart attack. I'm sorry, but I cannot save her. Where is your mother?"

"She is out working and will come back tonight," Ariana responded.

In the meantime, Don Nino and Salvatore arrived back home.

Don Nino touched Maria's feet and felt they were already cold. He said, "No! No! You too? I have already lost two wives, and now I'm losing you too. Is this my destiny?"

He turned to the doctor and said, "You cannot do anything to save her?"

The doctor responded, "I am sorry, but there is nothing that I can do for her. Stay with her and say goodbye; she could go any minute."

Ariana hugged her grandmother, and Maria died in her arms. Ariana was very attached to her grandmother. She could not believe she was dead. It was a shock to everybody.

Chapter 22

Everybody has their own destiny; when something is meant to happen, there is nothing anybody can do to change that.

The evening of Maria's death, the last thing Fortunata expected when she came home from work was to see her mother dead.

She got close to her, kissed her, and said, "Mamma, I love you so very much. I am sorry I was not here to tell you how much I loved you before you died. I love you very much, and I will really miss you. Mamma, I am in so much pain to lose you and will miss you very much."

Fortunata turned to the doctor and asked, "What has happened? You could not save her? I cannot believe that my Mamma is dead."

"Your daughter called me, and I came right away," the doctor said.

"As soon as I came, I noticed that she had a heart attack. She did not have the strength to say any words. The last thing she said to Ariana was that she had a headache, pain in her arm, and that she felt like she was going to vomit. She asked Ariana to call the doctor, which she did. I am sorry for you and your family, but since there is nothing for me to do, I must go. Goodbye, and God bless you all." And with that, the doctor left.

Don Nino made the preparations for the funeral, and after two days, the funeral took place.

The church was full of people, so full that there was no room for everyone inside, and people had to stand outside of the church.

People came from Porticello, where she was from. Everybody from San Nicola was there. All the friends of Don Nino and even the friends of the friends were there.

Everybody loved Maria because of all she did to help people. Everybody cried and said that God had gained an Angel.

Maria was so well loved and respected by everyone she had ever known. They called her "Mother Maria" for all the help that she gave to people.

After the church, everybody went to the cemetery where they were burying her, and for the last time, all the people who loved and respected her so much could say goodbye for the last time.

Everybody was sad because of how much they missed Maria every day, every week, every moment. Nobody even felt like smiling after she died.

A few days after the funeral, Don Nino went to the farm and chose a comfortable place to sit down and think. He started to think about his past and said, "I had three wives, and I loved all three of them dearly. Never in this world would I think I would remain alone when I became old. My God, what did I do to deserve this?"

He continued, "Maybe you are punishing me because I threw my son out of my house for not listening to me. I thought I was doing the right thing by demanding he live an honest life, but instead, he made his choice to continue to stay in the Mafia, so I refused to speak with him or even see him again. Or maybe it's because I agreed with my friend to kill my brother. If it was because of this, please forgive me. I did it to obey my father for the promise that we all made together before he died."

"I was proud of my father and kept the promise to work honestly without involvement in the Mafia. But my son, he disobeyed. And my brother, he disobeyed. Forgive me, God."

He started to think about when his first wife died on the trip to New York to see her family. She was expecting his first child.

He lost his second wife while she was also expecting, but with her last child, all because somebody gave her news that was not true, that her son Bastiano was dead from being trampled by a horse when he was lying still, scared. She left behind five children.

His third wife was brave and good. She raised his five children with respect, good intentions, and a good education.

Don Nino said to Maria, "Maria, you've been a very good wife and a very good second mamma for my five children. We stayed together for 40 years, and I did not expect that you would die before me."

He continued, "Maria, I am very tired and cannot continue without you. I will give my two sons, Salvatore and Antonino, my business and the remaining property. They can continue running the business as I was doing. For the wine, the oil, all the fruit and vegetables. I don't want to work anymore; I want to retire. I really love you. I will say goodbye, Maria. I hope I will see you again soon."

Maria died at 77 years of age.

Don Nino returned home and started to talk to Salvatore.

He said, "My son. I am very tired and have thought it is time to retire. I have taught you everything I know, and you have been doing an excellent job. I have much faith in you."

Don Nino continued, "I have decided to divide the farm where we have been making wine and the farm where we have been making oil, with fruit and vegetables. Half for you and half for Nino. Continue, and make me proud."

Salvatore responded, "Papa, I will say thank you, and I know what I am supposed to do. But regarding my brother, remember that he is a Finanziere."

He continued, "He is not here, so we do not know what he wants to do or if he wants to take care of the farm. You will need to talk to him first, and then we can see what we need to do."

"I know that you are tired. I want you to rest. Let's wait for my brother to come, and then we will talk to him," Salvatore said to his father.

Don Nino waited for the day his son came on vacation to discuss his retirement. When the day came, Don Nino also had a conversation with his son and Salvatore.

Nino responded to his father, saying, "Papa, I will not leave my job as a Finanziere. So, I would like to leave my brother to be in charge of everything. He can hire more men to help him, and I will pay the expenses. But I want my brother to take care of everything."

After hearing what Nino said, Don Nino and Salvatore agreed. From that day on, that is what they did, Nino paid the extra expenses so that Salvatore could manage all of the family businesses.

Don Nino spent the time with his friends who came to visit him. When they sold the wine in the winter, he would help Fortunata.

The remainder of Don Nino's life was to rest.

When the day would come that he believed he was going to die, he asked to see all his children, sons-in-law, daughters-in-law, and all his grandchildren. He wanted to see everybody in his family before he died.

He recognized everybody, mentioned each of them by name, and said to them all, "I want you all to respect each other, love each other, help each other, and work honestly. I pray God protects you all, my whole family."

Don Nino was not sick; he was always in good health. But he was very old now and exhausted.

He was ready to die, reunite with the wives that he loved, and spend eternity with his longest love, Maria.

His life ended at 99 years old.

Father and Sons

Melina Balistreri

About the Author

My name is Melina Balistreri, and I am the daughter of Fortunata Rizzo. I wrote the book "Love, Tragedy and Revenge," available on Amazon.com. I wrote this book, "Father and Sons," and I am writing a third book, which will be titled "The Power of Love." I now live in Las Vegas, after coming to America when I was 20 years old in 1963 on the ship Cristofer Columbo with my husband Salvatore Balistreri and my daughter Margherita, who was two and a half years old. After arriving in America, I had two other children, Maria Luisa and Marcello. I now have seven grandchildren and five great-grandchildren. The reason I am writing these books, which are all true stories, is to leave my family the story of where I came from, the remanent of my family in Sicily, the customs, and traditions, to better understand the sacrifice of how Sicily was before, how people used to dress, and how powerful the Mafia was.

Melina Balistreri

www.ingramcontent.com/pod-product-compliance
Lightning Source LLC
LaVergne TN
LVHW051950060526
838201LV00059B/3586